PRAISE FOR THE WRITING ~~OF~~ HIRSCH

WHAT MEN
DON'T
TELL WOMEN

Abby Hirsch
with Nancy Love

ST. MARTIN'S PRESS/NEW YORK

WHAT MEN DON'T TELL WOMEN

Copyright © 1989 by Abby Hirsch and Nancy Love.

ISBN: 0-312-91723-6 Can. ISBN: 0-312-91724-4

Printed in the United States of America

First St. Martin's Press mass market edition/October 1989

10 9 8 7 6 5 4 3 2 1

Acknowledgments

It will become clear to the reader of this book that I am deeply indebted to all of the men and women who have come to The Godmothers over the years for the stories and insights they have shared with me. Their pain and joy, their quibbles and triumphs have been the inspiration for the pages that follow.

I want to thank my associate, Andrea Farber, for her wisdom and inspiration. She has not only been able to glean information from male clients who are reluctant or unable to communicate easily—she also has a sixth sense about what they're *not* able to actually verbalize.

And my thanks, too, to Karin Keane, who also added valuable data on how men think and feel.

Introduction

In 1978 I opened a dating service called The Godmothers, Ltd., our slogan being: "What's success without romance." The service set out to attract as its clientele "the best and the brightest"—executive men and women who would never think of using a dating service.

The idea for The Godmothers was conceived at a dinner party in New York when a group of my friends—that emotionally deprived class that has everything except someone to share their success with—sat around bemoaning the fact that there was no one to fall in love with. Ten terrific men and ten terrific women were all in agreement that life was dull and gray without the possibility of that special someone to share a picnic with in the rain forest. This group wanted love, and yet there seemed to be no significant other on the horizon for any of them.

The hopelessly articulate, witty, and charming Manhattan bachelors at this dinner party had dropped their masks of cynicism and were talking about the desire for commitment, marriage, and children. It seemed most unusual. After all, these were the men who, not too long before, had equated wedlock with a bear trap.

For the women the words love, marriage, and phrases like "until death do us part" were the buzz words that had always melted like butterscotch on the tongue. Now, the men were uttering them too.

What did it mean?

I was determined to find out.

I elected myself the person to bring true love to the lives of hundreds of people like my successful friends. Within a month The Godmothers opened in New York. We had three "social management" account executives, four phone lines, and the Godmobile, a beautiful Austin Princess touring limousine that was sent to scoop up busy executives for their interviews. Because we were the first dating service catering only to executive high achievers, we were written about in magazines such as *New York* and *Fortune* as well as the New York daily newspapers. We appeared on national television talk shows and on local news telecasts.

Within a year I opened offices in Washington, D.C., and Philadelphia, and began to do "executive heart hunting"—custom-created campaigns to search for the state-of-the-art wife—on as many as three continents, as a service for our most affluent and demanding male clients.

I've learned a lot along the way, especially about the difference between what people say they want and what they really respond to. A few years ago I wrote a book called *The Lessons of Love* (William Morrow). It described my thesis that when people are truly available for relationships they usually find them—sometimes with a little help from a friend or a service like The Godmothers. And when they are not ready or interested in romantic attachments, they are destined to fail. I went to many cities to promote the book, often lecturing to large audiences of mostly women. I heard many stories about doomed attachments and impossible situations.

One beautiful twenty-eight-year-old architect sobbed as she told about coming home one day and finding a note from her live-in lover. It said, "I'm leaving. I've taken the stereo. You can have everything else." She couldn't understand what had happened. He would never return her calls to his office, so she never found out. "Up until the minute he left, I had no idea he was dissatisfied," she said. "I'm still in a state of shock. How could my judgment have been so bad? I'm afraid to get involved again."

Another client of ours told about falling in love at first sight. The man, handsome and elegant, was on the telephone she was waiting to use. He began to talk to her and was witty, warm, smart, and obviously a little drunk. "I wanted to know this man—I was captivated. I was also anxious to get back to my date who was waiting to leave. I excused myself. He kept talking. Finally, as I was walking away, he listed to the left and said, 'I can teach you how to never again get trapped by peer pressure.' I saw this man's life in front of me," she laughed, "every woman he'd kept waiting, every wife who'd ever left him."

I began to observe that men think, talk, and perceive relationships differently than women. When they say, "I'll call tomorrow," that's not what they mean at all. They just mean, "So long." But a woman takes it literally. When men hear the word wedlock, what they hear is bear trap. When a woman hears commitment, what she hears is opportunity.

I learned that men speak in different tongues—if they speak at all. I discovered men want to be perceived as strong and invulnerable, so it serves them well to remain mysterious. I was discussing the impostor principle with a man not too long ago. There had been a rash of books published about how women often thought they didn't deserve the promotions they got or any of the other good things that came their way. They thought they were putting something over on people, that they were impostors. Well, this guy said, "But that's *me*. I'm always afraid that someday someone is going to discover I don't really know what I'm talking about." When I started asking other men about this principle, I found that many of them thought they were impostors too. Another revelation about why so many men play it close to the vest.

John Updike wrote that American men are failed boys. Some never grew up to be the heroic figures they thought they would be. Some of them never grew up. But that's their secret.

When I asked one old friend what men don't tell women, he replied, "The truth." They don't exactly lie, but they may fudge the facts, polish the image, bury the naughty fantasy. Many men are always on guard with women. They aren't as relaxed as they are with the guys in the locker room. Obviously, they wouldn't tell you that they've been wanting to go to bed with your best friend, but they may be concealing something else they think you'd disapprove of, like how much black garter belts turn them on, or that they're afraid of dogs. Many men have never really been eager to be known in depth by women.

I also began to listen more carefully to the stories women told about men in their lives— the failure of past relationships that had brought them to The Godmothers. Then I started to ask men to tell us in greater detail about their failed romances, and how they had communicated their dissatisfaction to the women. What, if anything, had they done to work things out? How did they choose to end the relationship? How did they respond to endings they did not initiate? What, if any, changes did they plan to make in future relationships? What did they *really* want?

Men, I concluded, do not often tell women their real concerns. Left to figure things out for themselves, women can come to the wrong conclusions. They speculate about the way they think men will act or feel, and often what they are doing is projecting their own feelings onto the men.

At The Godmothers, men confide in us. They tell us what they are really looking for in a woman; they speak to us without any emotional editing about why former romances faded and why they couldn't, wouldn't, or didn't communicate what was in their hearts or heads to the woman in their lives. They feel free to talk to us more openly because we are neutral and impartial listeners—waitresses taking an order and trying to fill it.

Men and women often attach different meanings to the same words. There is a wide discrepancy in what they talk about and how they express it, in how they use the telephone, and what they expect to hear from another person. For instance, men are more competitive when they talk. They frequently interrupt and indulge in the kind of one-upmanship that can drive a woman crazy. They tend not to use the telephone as much for social chitchat as women do, and when a wife or girlfriend "visits" with a friend on the phone, it can drive *them* crazy.

After an introduction is arranged by The Godmothers, we ask for date reports from the couple. The purpose is to get both of them to tell us how the evening went, what they liked about the person or didn't. We ask, "What did you think about Mary? What do you think Mary thought about you?" Often, it's hard to believe that this man and woman were in the same place at the same time.

This book answers the questions most frequently asked by the women who've sought us out: "What do men really mean? What do they really look for? What do they really feel about money, sex, power? Why can't they express their feelings about all of these things?" We have found that, in general, women spend more time trying to figure out the meaning of men's actions and words than the other way around. This is due in part to our culture where it often becomes the responsibility of women to make intimate relationships work. Therefore, they need all the information they can get.

What Men Don't Tell Women attempts to demystify the American male. It's about why men are reluctant or unable to tell women what they are thinking. It deals with their real fears, true feelings, and the wide gap between what they say and what they mean.

• Chapter 1 •

Why Men Don't Talk to Women

Laura, a twenty-eight-year-old teacher, was complaining about the man we had fixed her up with. After three dates he was still an enigma to her. "I don't know why Seth won't talk to me," she was saying. "I keep making all these openings, but he avoids talking about anything personal. He's so withholding about his feelings. I just can't read him."

When I called him, Seth defended himself. "Listen, I don't know what she wants from me. She analyzes every sneeze. She's really into a lot of psychobabble about feelings. But... sometimes I just want to tell her to get lost."

He didn't tell Laura to get lost, and he didn't tell her that her need for constant play-by-plays of his nervous system was driving him crazy. He had fun with her and liked taking her places. He just wasn't up to turning on the kind of verbal intimacy she was demanding, so he just kept ducking the demands. To Seth it seems as if a woman like Laura can connect with her feelings in some magical way. The words flow from her body to her mouth without ever engaging her brain. He didn't want to make an issue of it, though. He just kept waiting for it to go away. But we passed on the word to Laura: "Cool it."

The need to respond on the kind of gut level Laura demanded can be like a body blow that literally immobilizes a big, strong, six-foot-four-inch man. The command to get in touch with his feelings might activate a futile search through his emotional file for a response he's not likely to locate during his next sip of margarita—or even after he's drained the entire glass. Or the need to perform emotional gymnastics can trigger a stubborn, hostile, or guilty response, and he retreats further behind his defenses. His guard is up. He goes on automatic avoidance. I know a man who turns on the radio in the car when he wants to escape probing forays by his wife. And I know some guys who conveniently fall asleep right after sex to avoid a post mortem.

• OFF LIMITS •

After Mark, a thirty-eight-year-old divorced corporation lawyer, had his third date with Helena—the bright sociologist I thought was perfect for him—I asked him how he was doing.

"I don't know," he said sadly. He'd spent a day at the beach with Helena. They took a picnic lunch, swam in the surf, collected shells. As far as he was concerned, they'd talked about many interesting things: a hot trial that was getting newspaper headlines every day, Wimbledon, dogs they had both owned. On the way home in the car, Helena was very quiet. Ominously quiet. The silence filled the car. Finally, she said, "We've been spending a lot of time together, but I don't know how you feel about me. I just can't get a reading."

"Look," Mark said to me, "I learned in my previous marriage that women keep expecting you to talk about your feelings for them all the time. This makes me feel real pressured and even guilty. But I just can't do it. Especially not with someone I'm not serious about yet. I'm just not a good bullshitter. I've only seen Helena a few times. I like what I've seen so far, but she just expects too much. I hate being put in that position."

Feelings in general are tough enough for men to discuss, but feelings about a woman are impossible until the right moment. Of all the things men complain about to me, pressure to declare intentions has got to be right up there in any top ten list of "worst things a woman can do."

What A Woman Can Do:

Resist the impulse to start discussions about how he feels about you until he's ready. He knows you want to hear this, and he'll get to it in his own good time. Maybe he's still not sure, and he knows if he doesn't say what you want to hear, he'll disappoint you, and he'll feel like a bad guy. Then there's the type who resents being asked before he's ready to deal with it. It's easier for him to skirt the issue. Your best strategy: Lighten up.

• BOYS DON'T CRY •

Many men are trying harder to get in touch with their feelings. "That's one of the things I've learned from the feminists in my life," a successful young attorney confided in me. "It's amazing how much better I feel if I can cry like I did when my dog died last year. I mean, that was a breakthrough for me. I can act hurt or disappointed instead of pretending to be cool and brave. My mental health has really improved." But not all men are candidates for sensitivity training.

There is a definite difference in the ability of men and women to plug into their emotions. We've been programmed differently. It goes back to the way boys and girls are brought up. It's all right for girls to cry, to baby their dolls, to be babied themselves. Girls discover boys at an earlier age than boys discover them, and right from the start they compare notes with their girlfriends. No one teaches them, but they pick up on how to communicate their thoughts and feelings as they experience them. Confiding and being confided in becomes second nature.

Little boys, on the other hand, as we all know, have to blink back the tears when they fall down or lose the game. You're a sissy if you're afraid. Real boys don't show their feelings or talk about them. Boys are much older than girls when they become overtly attracted to the opposite sex. When they start to talk to other boys about dates, it's usually about whether or not—and to what extent—they "made out." As they grow from boys to men, they get almost no practice in accessing their emotional lives, or in talking about them.

By contrast, think of what women usually experience as they grow up. Even their teenage magazines and books explore ten ways to tell whether you're in love and how to survive heartbreak. By the time they graduate to *Cosmopolitan* and the current crop of how to live a lifetime in ten minutes books, they are already experts. They study their own reactions, they get feedback from their friends, they work on perfecting their skills in the management of their own emotions, and the art of detecting the status of everyone else's.

Consciousness-raising groups were a natural for women. The idea of sitting around airing feelings of hate, love, and inadequacy, of taking apart lover, boss, or husband in front of a room full of peers, felt good to women. Just articulating gripes, terrors, and guilt was an instant catharsis. But beyond that, there was the reinforcement of knowing that others had the same problems, that you were not alone, and the advice and positive support women received from the group.

Although most of the original women's movement consciousness-raising groups have vanished, they have spawned the eighties' equivalent in colleges and on the job. One group of female law students met informally in the school cafeteria at lunchtime to compare notes on how much trouble they had studying for the last exam because a lover kept demanding attention. Female architects in a large firm where they are a tiny minority try to meet for drinks after work a few times a month to bolster each other's morale.

There have been successful male consciousness-raising groups, but the idea never caught on the way it did with women. I've heard from some men that after they got through with women bashing, there didn't seem to be much else to talk about, and the meetings would turn into gripe sessions.

• HIDDEN MESSAGES •

There is another reason communication between men and women can be a mine field of grief and misunderstanding. Men can't always express what they're thinking. They know what's going on in their heads and somehow they expect women to be able to absorb the message by osmosis. I was called in to mediate when one of my couples got their unspoken messages mixed.

Sidney is a promising biochemist who underestimates his attractiveness to women. He had dated Joanne, a headhunter with her own business, about five or six times, but when he called for the next date, she was busy. He didn't set up another date.

Then his back acted up, and he was a semi-invalid for the next few weeks. During this period, Joanne called to invite Sidney to a party. He told her his back was really bad, and he wasn't up to a party. She didn't call again.

That made Sidney mad. He told us, "I expected to hear from Joanne. What kind of a friend is she, if she didn't care enough to call to find out how I was, or to offer to go out and get a newspaper for me?" After a week of stewing, he called Joanne and bawled her out. Then Joanne got mad and confused.

"When I invited Sid to the party, he didn't say he was sorry he couldn't go, and that he'd like to see me when he felt better. So I decided he didn't really want to see me again. I didn't like risking rejection again, so I didn't follow up."

We soothed her hurt feelings, and explained that Sidney had misread her silence. "He thought, 'I'm uncomfortable and in pain. If Joanne liked me, she'd pay some attention to me instead of ignoring me.' So, if you want to see him again, call and apologize."

What A Woman Can Do:

Men often assume people know what they mean even when they don't put the thought into words. They are not accustomed to articulating their needs, to asking someone to do something for them. Many of them think women can interpret their unspoken cries for attention the way their mothers did.

If you think the man in your life wants something from you, ask him. Why guess? Or, if you care about him, make sure that what you are assuming is a brushoff, really is one. If Joanne could have overcome her fear of rejection, and said, "I'm sorry you're not feeling well enough to go out tomorrow night, but if you'd like, I can stop by on my way to the party to say hello. Or would you rather be left alone?" That would have put the ball back in Sidney's court. He would have known Joanne was concerned about him and it would have given him the cue to ask her to check in with him again.

• BRIDGING THE CONVERSATION GAP •

Do you sometimes feel that men and women aren't talking the same language? We've all had the experience of men saying at the end of a date, "I'll call you tomorrow." You learn quickly that a man's "I'll call you tomorrow," means "See you around." Women tend to be more literal than men about these social niceties. The language of men is given to hyperbole, obfuscation, and circumlocutions when they are trying to communicate with the opposite sex.

"You're beautiful without your glasses," means, "Women who wear glasses are bookish and therefore trouble. I can deal with you better when you take them off." Or, "I want you to look good for my friends. Keep the glasses off." When a man says he's weak, he's warning you that he's not a one-woman man. If he says he's shy, he's telling you not to push him too fast sexually.

Women are quick to pick up the wrong signals. They tend to read more into simple courtesies or statements of fact than men intend. Women who pick up a word and run with it are busy creating scripts with themselves in the starring role, while the reality might be that they are still bit players. When he says he likes children, it doesn't necessarily mean that he wants to have children with *you*. Men tell me that women seize on perfectly innocuous social niceties and blow them up into Significant Signs. When he asks you which restaurant you want to go to for dinner, he's not saying, "I love you." He's not even treating you in a special way. He's just being polite.

So, if it often seems to you that men and women are using two different communications systems, experts agree. They are. Psychologists Mark Sherman and Adelaide Haas began to ask questions about conversations men had with other men and women had with other women. They discovered that what men talk about with other men, and the way they do it, is quite different from the way women communicate with each other. No wonder that when men and women try to talk to each other, there is so much chaos.

Think about the difference in the way most men and most women use the telephone. Men make phone calls to get or give information. Even a call that isn't for business is usually brief, fast-paced, and to the point. Women use the phone for quickies, too, but they also use it to chat with friends. A man's call, even a social call, has a purpose. A woman's social call might not.

It drives a lot of men crazy when their wives, girlfriends, or daughters have long, rambling telephone visits with their friends or their mothers. "What can you talk about for so long?" they gripe. Or, "You talked to her yesterday, what could you still have to say?"

As Sherman and Haas point out, most of us rarely hear the private conversations of the other sex. We don't know what they are talking about, how they are saying it, or why. We approach conversations with members of the opposite sex with the same expectations we have for conversations with members of our own sex. But, trust me, they are not the same.

If you listen in, you will find that conversations between men fall into three categories: Small talk ("Did you see the Mets game last night!"), giving and receiving practical advice ("Let me tell you about this new stock offering."), and showing off ("Man, did I clean up on that deal!"). Men tend to be competitive when they talk. They fight for the floor. They interrupt. They don't always listen, because they're so busy thinking of what to say next.

Women enjoy trivial chitchat, too, but they also want support and sympathy from their friends and relatives. Women pay attention to each other, and make an effort to understand. More often than not, they tend to give advice when it's asked for, instead of barging in and taking over.

But when men and women try to talk to each other, there is often a clash of styles. They are each playing by a different set of rules and there's no umpire.

Stacy comes home from work and starts to say, "Linda seems to be ignoring me lately. I really don't understand..."

Her husband Hal interrupts with, "Listen, I think you worry about her too much. Just forget it."

Stacy is hurt. She wants to talk office politics. She hates it when Hal interrupts her, and when he gives her advice she didn't ask for. What she wants is a sympathetic ear.

Hal isn't particularly interested in this line of discussion, which will meander on and never really get anywhere. He blurts out his honest reaction, and then realizes that he's somehow hurt Stacy's feelings again.

What Hal Expects: Hal is looking for the playfulness and camaraderie he enjoys with his male friends. His conversations tend to stay on the surface of emotions. He likes not having to watch what he says as often as he does with Stacy. With men, he might solve practical problems or explore common agendas, but it's unlikely that he'd get mired in sticky, insoluble personal problems.

What Stacy Expects: Stacy is used to conversations that might be practical and fun at times, but may at other times lead to self-understanding and to understanding others. She's used to an empathetic listener. Hal has let her down again by cutting her off with advice she didn't want.

What A Woman Can Do:

Just knowing that men and women communicate differently relieves some of the tensions. I've seen it happen with my clients. If Stacy understood that Hal is impatient because she's talking about a co-worker, which isn't exactly a high priority topic for men, she wouldn't take his abruptness so personally. And if she knew that he always interrupts her because that's the preferred way for men to get the floor, she'd understand that he's not attacking her. That's just the style he's used to and is most comfortable with.

I tell women to sensitize themselves to these annoying conversational habits, and to try to recognize a pattern. It's amazing how much more tolerant you can be when you realize that something like interrupting is a common ploy in male conversation, and has nothing to do with you.

That doesn't mean you shouldn't ask a man to try to change. If his constant interruptions are bugging you, point out in a calm way: "I know you don't realize how I feel when you interrupt me the way you just did. It makes me feel you don't want to hear what I have to say, that you don't care about my opinions."

He will probably be contrite, and try not to do it, especially if you tell him matter-of-factly without putting him on the defensive. But don't expect miracles. He'll probably drift back to his old style and need more coaching.

You might also try to figure out what you do conversationally that bothers the man in your life, and attempt to modify your own behavior. If he really doesn't like to hear you discuss problems about your friends and co-workers, save those topics for your female confidantes.

• DANGER ZONE •

Jeff was saying to me the other day, "Why isn't it as easy to talk to the women I'm dating, as it is to talk to my men friends? We just keep having these little blowups about nothing." Jeff is twenty-eight. He's learning that intimacy can foul up the lines of communication as nothing else can.

Roger is thirty-five, and he's figured it out. He says, "In the beginning it's easy to communicate with women, but they're like accountants counting the times you say something they want to hear. Like they keep ledgers."

I press him to be more explicit. He continues, "When you first meet a woman, you can talk about anything. You can tell her about your past relationships, how you feel about having kids, or what you want to do with the rest of your life. But then it changes. Everything becomes emotionally charged.

"She starts to be jealous about the other women in your life, so you can't talk about that. If she wants children and she's over thirty, watch out. She'll start dropping it into the conversation, and get all dewy-eyed. I find myself not answering. You know, I sort of freeze up, because some of these questions are things that she has more than a casual interest in. They're loaded. I don't want her to expect too much."

Maybe Roger overreacts to harmless stimuli, but probably not. Men develop a sixth sense about entrapment, about triggering unrealistic expectations. Nothing can kill fun and spontaneity faster than suddenly finding that a harmless conversation is leading into unsafe territory.

One of my clients, who had moved to Washington from Minneapolis recently, told me he used to invite women to his apartment for dinner, but women in Washington thought he was "serious" when he did that. He likes to cook, so it was no big deal for him to throw a dinner together. But he was looking for new friends, not a lifetime commitment when he issued an invitation. Dinner at his place meant something else to women. He found himself being emotionally and/or sexually pressured by the end of those evenings, which are now a thing of the past.

• CRACKING THE CODE •

Instant intimacy is the stuff of novels and fantasy. If a man is sending confusing messages, perhaps there's a good reason for it in the early stages of a relationship, when neither party should want to force an issue because of the risk of being hurt or misunderstood. Better to leave it ambiguous than step into a forbidden zone of unexplored possibilities.

Judith Sills, Ph.D., says in her book *A Fine Romance*, "Honest self-disclosure is at the core of intimacy. It's what we're all working toward. But it can't be rushed. To help intimacy along, coded messages can be used to convey important information in a way that makes it easier to accept."

What does it mean when a man always insists that a woman spend the night at his place, not at hers? He always has an excuse. He's expecting a call. He won't have time to go home to change his clothes in the morning. Does it mean he doesn't like her apartment? Is he one of those people who sleeps better in his own bed? Does he feel he's too vulnerable

29

if he's on her turf? Or are his given excuses legitimate?

Jeanne, one of our clients, had dated Schuyler a few times. She was filled with anxiety when he asked her to go to a party his sister was giving. She called us with a million questions. Did that mean Schuyler was in love with her? Was she on trial? Did it mean he wanted feedback from his family? It has been our experience that a man is probably playing it safe at this stage in a relationship. Chances are it was a casual invitation, and Schuyler attached no particular importance to it. He wanted to bring a date because everyone else was. On the other hand, he might be starting to like Jeanne enough to risk introducing her to members of his family, to see how she fits in. If so, he might not have even admitted that to himself.

The difference between men and women is that women spend more time trying to crack the code to decipher the hidden messages. What does it mean if he suddenly stops dating you on Saturday night, and asks to switch to Friday night? Is it just more convenient for him that week on a Friday? Is he seeing someone else?

What does it mean when he says he likes you in blue? Does it mean that blue is flattering to you, or that he didn't like you in that red dress you wore the last time you saw him?

I've seen men close to apoplexy because the woman of the moment is examining every word and nuance for a sign. Better they should stick to reading palms or tea leaves. They probably wouldn't jump to so many wrong conclusions. Steven and Rhoda, both in their mid-thirties, have been dating a few months. He's said a few times when the subject has come up that he'd like to have children. Rhoda began to probe more deeply. Marriage and children are a high priority for her. She wants to start a family as soon as possible. Since Steven seemed amenable to the idea of a family, she began to assume he was anxious to get married, too.

In reality, he hadn't made up his mind about her yet. He told us he had been far from deciding whether or not they were right for each other. In her false euphoria about the stage of the relationship, Rhoda pushed too hard. She ended up scaring Steven away by adding up two and two and getting five.

What A Woman Can Do:

Don't rush things. Psychologists like Judith Sills warn us that although we feel we are understanding a situation, especially at the start of a relationship, what is more likely is that we are projecting our own anxieties and feelings onto that situation. Rhoda read more into Steven's discussion about children than he intended. She imagined he was ready to propose marriage because that's how *she* felt.

Learn to live with ambiguities. Don't rush things. Have other activities that don't depend on him. Give the relationship time to grow and mature on its own without too much interference. As you discover more about each other, you will find more clues to understanding his coded communication. With time, if the relationship is going to flourish, both of you will begin to open up more.

• UNHAPPY ENDINGS •

Endings can be as tricky as beginnings. When relationships are in trouble, why won't men talk about what's going on? They often just walk out. No conversation. No explanation. One woman told me that when she called the man in another city she had dated for two years because she hadn't heard from him, he said, "Didn't you get my letter?" "What letter?" she asked. "The letter I sent to tell you I wasn't going to be able to see you anymore."

She had suspected that he had started seeing a woman in his office, so the break didn't come as a complete surprise. "But," she told me, "he doesn't get to do it on the phone. Or through the mail. After two years he owed me an explanation—and in person. I had to drag it out of him. The new woman had decreed that he could never see me again, not even as a friend. All my former lovers are still my friends. This was ridiculous."

"I just can't stand the thought of having an emotional confrontation," Sean, thirty, a furniture restorer, told me when he explained that he wasn't enjoying his relationship with Melanie anymore. I was trying to talk him into going to Melanie with a list of things he'd like to fix between them, and suggestions for how they could do it. "It sounds all right, but it's not going to work. Somehow, I know it'll all be my fault, and nothing will be resolved. I just want to drop the whole thing." Sean was not going to be persuaded to try to work on the relationship.

When a relationship is in trouble, a woman often asks for a chance to talk it through. But when a man hears those words, the first thing he thinks of is big trouble. He's sure he's headed for a dreaded confrontation where he's going to be in the wrong. In his business life, he's used to discussing a problem and settling it quickly. In his personal life, his experience is that often resolution is slow, painful, and never really complete. But he doesn't tell a woman what his fears are. Like Sean, he will probably fold his tent and disappear into the night.

What A Woman Can Do:

One of the mistakes we observe is women attacking or nagging indiscriminately, without a strategy in mind when things are going badly in a relationship. He's unhappy, and if you really think about it, you probably know why. Take a guess. That's better than asking him why he's unhappy. It is important to try to isolate the problem in advance, and then to think of possible solutions. If you need his input, take a page from the lingua franca of the business world and consider negotiation.

Here are some of the basics:

1. Think win-win. If what you want is an ongoing relationship, it's foolish to aim for win-lose. You do not want to win at his expense. You can only hurt yourself in the long run because he'll resent losing. Forget that. You can both be winners.

2. What's in it for you? What's in it for him? Think through problems that way. Neither person has to compromise if you consider the big picture. He needs more time to himself; you want more time with him. The big picture is that if you can work it out, you will continue to have time together, and you will enjoy your time together more. If you can manage to satisfy both of you, you both win.

3. Be creative. Stop trying to convince him he's wrong and you're right, and come up with a fresh point of view. Tell him you have a great idea you want to present to him. That should disarm him and put him in a good mood. Let's say you've thought of alternate weekends at your place and at his. Whoever is the host for the weekend gets to decide what you both do. You might see less of him on his weekends because he might choose to spend the afternoon practicing the guitar or going to the library, but there will

still be some shared time, and on the weekend you host, you can have it all your way.

4. If he vetoes the idea, maybe it will inspire him to think of a better one. At least it won't start another round of who's right and who's wrong. That's a guaranteed no win for both of you.

• MOST COMMON COMMUNICATION COMPLAINTS •

One of the most common complaints we get from men is that women don't pay enough attention to them. Everyone is so busy and distracted, but the best way to attract someone, and to find out whether or not you are attracted to him, is to take a few deep breaths, settle down, and just try to get to know him. Forget who just walked into the party, or what you're going to wear to the wedding tomorrow. Focus all your powers of communication on him.

Being there works; playing grand inquisitor doesn't. A brainy businessman with a list of interests that range from opera to oenology complained that the woman we fixed him up with, who was also in retailing, kept interrogating him about business. He said, "After awhile, I felt as if I were out on some business deal, not a date."

What A Woman Can Do:

You are trying to conduct a conversation, not an interview, so don't go about it as if your life—or your job—depended on it. If you are genuinely interested in this man, he will begin to respond without your prying information out of him.

Of course, ask questions, but not ones that can be answered yes and no. Make them open-ended enough so that he can rattle on by himself without constant prodding. Give him plenty of time to finish what he's trying to say. There's nothing more disconcerting than having some bright-eyed person coiled ready to spring before the words are even out of your mouth. As they say in the theater, "Don't step on his lines." He might want to think, comment, or move out of the question-and-answer mode.

Other common complaints:

1. "Sit down, I want to talk to you," is an instant turnoff. A man immediately thinks he's been caught doing something he shouldn't be doing, or that he'll hear something that will be upsetting.
2. Other phrases men hate: "Meaningful relationship," "Am I wasting my time?" and the word "sensitivity."
3. Men tell me, "There's a certain pitch, a tone of voice, I don't want to hear." When some women get information they don't like, their voices go up, become shrill and penetrating. If a man stops listening

when he hears that timbre, you've lost him.

4. "I guess she really gets around, but all that name-dropping was wasted on me. I hate it when women talk on and on about people I don't know."

5. "I don't want to hear a woman badmouth her ex-husband or ex-lover."

6. Men don't want to hear about the state of your health. Don't discuss your past or current headache, menstrual cramps, or that you get an average of fourteen colds a year.

7. They don't want to listen to women talk about their business lives, and they don't want to be interrogated about what they do.

• THE BOTTOM LINE •

Although the battlefields have changed, the battle between the sexes is still being waged all over America at this very moment. Women have more weapons today, but the tongue is still mightier than the sword. It is on the communication level that most of the skirmishes on the road to love will be won or lost.

There will continue to be misunderstandings and miscommunications. Women can try to anticipate, placate, and avoid unnecessary trauma, but ultimately men bring to each encounter their own mindsets that will color all of their conversations with the opposite sex.

These are the secrets they keep to themselves, until they are ready to share them.

If they are frightened or uncomfortable with the idea of an ongoing relationship, that will set the tone for their communication. If, on the other hand, they think of a relationship as a solution to their own personal problems, they will approach it more openly.

The trick is to know where he's coming from without actually forcing the issue. I will always remember the man who complained that his last live-in had been the type who wanted to talk out everything. "I was so talked out that I was exhausted all the time. Maybe it was because she was so verbal. But please get me someone who doesn't think communicating means taking a reading on every heartbeat." Talking has its limitations!

• Chapter 2 •

Who's In Charge Here?

A forty-year-old woman sits in my office and tells about the final power struggle that made her decide to leave her husband. They ran a tax shelter company that specialized in film deals. She was the president and he was the chief operating officer. But he was constantly trying to muscle her out of decisions. One day he insisted on conducting an important meeting without her being in on it. She went into the bathroom and spent an hour trying to set the silk wallpaper on fire.

The old territorial system that predetermined the spheres of influence of males and females has broken down. Gone are the days when it was agreed that men worked and women took care of the home and children, and that the breadwinner had the final say on how the bread was dispersed. Men decreed and women deferred. Oh, women did a lot of unacknowledged manipulation, and if they got really out of line, people said their husbands were henpecked.

It is no longer assumed that man's place is on top—literally or figuratively. Now most women work and some men stay at home. Women have an acknowledged right to sexual pleasure and men have a right to an active role in childrearing. Both men and women bring home the bacon, and either one may cook it. Every center of power and decision-making is up for grabs. And this is bringing long-buried issues out of the closet.

Men tell us they want women who work, but not women with careers, or I've had a man say, "I'm tired of women who keep trying to be macho." They have this ambivalence about how much power they're willing to give up. Women are ambivalent, too. A lot of them are uneasy with their newfound power.

In my experience, if men have the illusion of freedom to do what they please, they have the illusion of power. As long as they can call the shots, they are happy. If someone tries to take this illusion of power away from them, they begin to feel helpless and grow angry and resentful. They hunker down and plot to get back in control.

Women don't want to roll over and play dead either. Most of them don't ask for total control, but they've tasted freedom, too, and they're not going to back down that easily. The greatest dilemma for women is that they need a power base in a relationship, because that's how they will have some freedom and autonomy, but if they win that battle, they risk losing the man.

• THE UPPER HAND •

Most people are constantly struggling with their need to control other people. The real difference between the mature and immature is the ability to edit their behavior. A CEO of a cosmetics firm spent an hour in my office telling me about his former girlfriend. When he suspected her of cheating on him, he hired detectives. They found that she had run off for a discreet evening with another man. He said, "I was furious. Not because I loved her so much, but because things felt out of control." To right the balance, he arranged to have $100,000 worth of jewelry he had given her "stolen." Then he felt he was in control again.

Men tell The Godmothers they are willing to *share* power. But to what extent? Many men seem to have a need to be secure about how much control they're holding onto. These are the guys who tell us in ways that they think are subtle, that sure they want an independent woman—as long as she stays in line. A twenty-nine-year-old engineer from the Midwest said to me, "In New York the women seem to be so pushy and aggressive. I go to Europe on business a lot, and there's a difference. American women are much more controlling."

What men like this seem to be saying is, Yes, I want a bright, with-it woman, but I don't want one who will try to control me. In their book *Women Men Love—Women Men Leave*, authors Dr. Connell Cowan and Dr. Melvyn Kinder point out that men need to be in charge to bolster their own sense of security. When they fall in love with a woman, their emotional dependency on her causes conflicts within them. They worry that the attachment and need for this woman will weaken and engulf and overwhelm them, so they struggle to maintain their equilibrium.

Whatever the psychological reasons, men often tell us that they hate feeling controlled or manipulated. If they perceive that they are being pushed in ways they are uncomfortable with, they might become stubborn and uncommunicative. A man may not express his anger because he's afraid it will threaten the relationship. Instead, he becomes silently resentful, especially if he caves in, in an effort to please the woman. We fixed up the engineer who didn't like overly aggressive women with an illustrator we thought would be just right for him. She was a willowy blonde with an ingenuous smile who wore flowered skirts and had an easy, laid-back manner. On their first date, he suggested a restaurant. She said that sounded fine, but then came up with a list of alternatives. "Okay," he said, "you make the choice." Then she said, "We'd better go with your original suggestion, because that's the one you'd really prefer."

At the restaurant he picked a wine. She agreed, but began thinking of other possibilities. Maybe something a little drier, or maybe an Italian wine would go better with the food they had chosen. "Whatever you want," he said. "Oh, no," she protested. "You'd probably rather have the one *you* suggested."

It was like this with everything they did. She always said she'd go along with whatever he wanted, but she'd pick holes in every idea. Then she'd take a stand, and once again take it back. He liked her and found her fun to be with, but this aspect of her personality made him uneasy.

After the first date or two, he stopped making suggestions. He began to ask her first what *she* wanted, and then he'd go along with that. It was easier. Although he didn't say anything about it, he felt used and impotent. His resentment grew, and finally, after the fourth date, he told us he wasn't going to see her anymore.

What A Woman Can Do:

If you have wishes and desires, make them clearly understood. At least, that way they're on the table. But every small decision can't be blown up into a power play.

• SMOTHER LOVE •

Many women also fear loss of control in a relationship. They need the same kind of security that men need. But where a man may just walk away when he feels too uncomfortable, a woman may act—often obliquely—to redress the balance. A woman who feels powerless may resort to techniques like snooping, finding fault, or being unreasonably demanding, to bolster her sense of security.

Their dates may not complain to them, but they call The Godmothers and say, "This woman is pushy, bossy, and miserable. My car isn't new enough, my friends aren't successful enough, she is entitled to more conversation from me, why don't I spend more time with her." If you are a man getting that kind of treatment, your inclination will be to run, or to fight, and then run.

We had fixed up a hardworking editor with the owner of a boutique—with killer hours herself—who began to disapprove of the time he spent playing tennis. "She's telling me that, if I didn't play tennis on weekends, we'd be able to see more of each other," he told us plaintively. "I really like her and want to spend time with her, but she has to understand that I *need* the tennis. If I didn't have that, I think I'd go out of my mind. It's my safety valve."

She cooled it after a phone call from us warning her that she was going to lose her man altogether if she made him choose between her and tennis.

We also hear about the woman who sets herself up as a surrogate mother and preempts a power position by making the man need her. She cooks lavish dinners, offers to babysit with his children, sends cute letters and greeting cards, is always available when he wants her—and even when he doesn't.

He is smothered with kindness, and suddenly worries that she is taking over his life. One of our new clients told us her last relationship had ended so mysteriously and abruptly, that she was still in shock. She'd been seeing an accountant six nights a week. At their last meeting, he'd come to her apartment for dinner. She'd cooked all his favorites, as she loved to do—lamb chops, double-baked potatoes, asparagus, raspberry pie—and he'd eaten every last morsel of raspberry pie before he told her that he had met another woman and was going to marry her.

"How could he have eaten the whole dinner before telling me?" she wanted to know. "And how did he have time to meet and fall in love with another woman? He only had Monday nights." She thought she could control him with her gifts of food and attention, and by monitoring every aspect of his social life.

Another common variety of smotherer that men complain to us about is the woman who begins to check up on them. She tracks his activities by telephone when he's supposed to be at home or at the office, by sneaking looks at his engagement calendar, by asking probing questions about what he's doing when he's not with her. When the relationship is getting closer, she tightens the screws even more. The man is getting more ambivalent and perhaps set for flight at any moment, so the woman escalates her surveillance.

This kind of overpossessiveness is often triggered by jealousy. Is he seeing other women? Is he *thinking* of seeing other women? Putting a man on the defensive about his personal life can have a chilling effect on his feelings toward you. If he still wants to work things out with you, your suspicions could be the kiss of death.

Control Quiz

How do you know when you are becoming domineering and overly controlling? Men will tell us, but they are probably not telling you. This quiz can give you some insights.

Answer the following statements True or False.

1. I usually have to do most of the work in a relationship.
2. Men I am interested in are often intimidated by me.
3. I expect praise from the man in my life for what I do for him.
4. I hate to have anyone help me when I'm cooking.
5. I never have any doubts that my decisions are the right ones.
6. I am uneasy when my boyfriend takes a trip without me.
7. Most things that go wrong with our relationship are his fault.

8. It is essential that I win every argument with my lover.
9. I like to know where my partner is at all times.
10. I try to anticipate his needs and desires and arrange everything without asking him.

To Score:

0–2 Trues. You are not controlling and have no trouble sharing power.

3–5 Trues. Control might be a problem for you. You are unlikely to want to let anyone share power with you.

6–10 Trues. It is difficult for you to trust a man. You are happy only when you are in charge.

What A Woman Can Do:

If you suspect that you are fussing over a man too much, becoming too possessive, or are overly controlling, you should be alert to signs of hidden hostility on his part. Maybe he *wants* you to have the power position, but if he doesn't, he might not express his dissatisfaction openly.

Here are some danger signals to watch for: He agrees to your suggestions, but doesn't really act on them. He's on the defensive and seems to be challenged all the time. He isn't as enthusiastic about sex as he once was.

Try to talk about what's happening. This may not be easy (see Chapter One), but the one who desires a change is the one who has to initiate it. You might have to rely on your instincts and good sense.

If you have a hunch that you are reminding him too much of his mother or other women in his life who pressured and nagged, perhaps you can forgo a discussion. Let go a bit. Stand back and give him more space. Try to be more trusting. He won't love you because you demand it. If he does really love you, he will welcome the opportunity to show he does on his own—without prompting from you. No one can be coerced into being faithful or into giving up autonomy. A person who doesn't want to be pushed will take it for only so long.

• WE CAN'T HAVE TWO LEADERS •

How about men who want to be in charge all the time? Marshall is a business broker who knows his way around. When it comes to women, all he has to do is say, "We can't both be leaders. I'm the leader, you're the follower," and they'll follow him anywhere.

Men who are used to having great power in their working world or in their civic lives, often expect to have that much control in all situations. Professional army officers like the Great Santini—who ran his children and wife as if they were Army recruits—assume the same role at home that they've had in the barracks.

Or the opposite might be true. A hardworking doctor we know doesn't want to make decisions or exercise control once he's off duty. He's been making life-and-death decisions all day. Once he stops working, he doesn't want the responsibility for any more decisions. The women in his life have to make all social arrangements, pay the bills, and even decorate his homes and offices.

This is the kind of man who comes to us and says, "I want an independent woman," and means it. He doesn't want a woman who will lean on him, or a woman he has to take care of. After all, the one who has all the power has all the responsibility as well, and that's not a prospect everyone looks forward to.

When I hear "independent woman" I imagine a woman who thinks for herself, has her own job and interests, her own style and persona, knows something about handling money, can keep herself busy and occupied, and is not dependent on a man for every social move. Being independent does not mean you are a controlling woman who has to run the whole show. Most men don't want someone who will plan their lives for them and then expect them to follow the plan, no questions asked.

And most men aren't looking for a woman who wants a man to mold her or take care of her, either. I recently interviewed a new client who said to me, "I can't tell my former girl-friend why I left her. Her life was a mess, so I found her a lawyer, an accountant, a dentist. I was doing job counseling and amateur therapy twenty-four hours a day. I'm forty-two years old. I'm happy to help someone, but I don't want full responsibility for them."

It is important for a woman to know where she fits into the independent-dependent equation, the lead-or-be-led scenario. Are you going to be happy with the man who wants to be the leader, the one who *doesn't* want to be the leader, or with someone who wants to share leadership?

A woman who was dating the I-am-your-leader business broker Marshall was a successful business woman who had a lot of self-confidence. When he would say, "We can't have two leaders," she'd hold her tongue. But she'd quietly go about finding other ways to assert herself. She wasn't about to roll over and play dead. This was a source of continuing friction between them until they finally broke up.

What we found for Marshall was a low-keyed, California type. She worked in an art gallery, had no long-range career goals or need to assert herself. She always seemed to get along by going along. Her ability to be both trusting and enthusiastic played well with Marshall. The fact that she agreed to an unspoken noncompete clause was an extra bonus.

Who is the right woman for the doctor who wants to go off duty when he leaves his office? Why, a woman like Marshall, of course, someone who enjoys being in charge. She has fought the battle for independence, first with her own parents, and then with her teachers and bosses...and maybe a few boyfriends. She has reached a level of autonomy and confidence that is comfortable for her. Under the right circumstances, she'd be happy to take over.

• THE SHIFTING BALANCE OF POWER •

In ongoing relationships the power often shifts. At times it seems that one person has all the power, then it changes. The catalyst could be a major life change. He gets a promotion and is suddenly earning more than she does. He starts to call the shots—how they entertain, where they go to dinner, what friends they cultivate.

Or if they started with a tutor-pupil relationship and she catches up to her mentor, she begins to shop alone for clothes, plan her own trips, and assume responsibility for her own life. Everything was fine as long as she depended on him for guidance. Now everything is different.

At The Godmothers we keep track of couples and watch these situations evolve. A common one starts with the man pursuing the woman. When he gets her, his attention wanders, and she starts to pursue him. Harry was forty and needy when he met Louise. He'd had a nasty divorce, missed his children, and his business partner had left, taking some major clients with him. Louise came to represent sanity and stability. She was a college professor in sociology, had two teenage children and a lively circle of friends.

At first, Louise was less interested than Harry, but gradually, in response to his ardent wooing, she began to fall for him. His offers of marriage sounded better and better. Eight months later, life had stabilized for Harry and he didn't need Louise in the same way. The balance of power began to shift. Louise became uneasy. Harry wasn't as dependent on her and her close circle of family and friends for support. She stopped seeing her friends and concentrated more on Harry. She began to cling, to berate him for not calling as often, to insist that he come to dinner when it wasn't convenient for him, to make him feel guilty for missing a school play her son was in.

Harry finally withdrew altogether. That brought Louise to her senses. She pulled herself together and went back to her former lifestyle. She realized she had gotten too possessive and controlling with Harry and determined never to make that mistake again. One night she bumped into Harry at a concert, and they went out for coffee afterward. Louise, her old relaxed self, admitted to him that she understood now what she had done to their relationship. He realized how much he missed her, and they started to see each other again, cautiously at first as they felt their way to a better balance of power.

One superbright charmer—a Harvard Law School graduate in his late thirties who loved to travel, hike, and paint watercolors—told us he wanted a smart, independent woman who didn't want children. We produced what we thought would be the girl of his dreams. She was an interior designer with her own business, she enjoyed the outdoors, and made it quite clear that she wasn't interested in starting a family.

It seemed like love at first sight. Over their first drink he told her, "I've been waiting for you all my life." They were inseparable from then on. Until a strange thing began to happen. He started to cut down on how often he saw her. He seemed remote and distracted. She tried harder to please him, but he complained often about her shortcomings. He turned from the ultimate romantic into the most demanding perfectionist. He loved being able to make demands on her. And then it became obvious what his game was. He said he wanted a relationship, but what he really wanted was for it to fail. To him, having power means never having to make a commitment.

What A Woman Can Do:

Rule #1. Don't panic if a man starts to back off after he's come on strong and won your heart.

Rule #2. Don't start pursuing him. The only course of action is to play it cool and size up the situation.

Rule #3. Back off, too. Don't call him or initiate meetings. Don't be available all the time. Don't scold him for his lack of attention. Playing hard to get might be difficult, but think of it as a temporary strategy that you'll try for a week or two. If the experiment doesn't work, you can always switch back to a more aggressive stance.

Who pursues whom is always an interesting question. Generally speaking, men want to be able to take the initiative. Oh, they say they like the idea of being asked out by a woman, but as one man was truthful enough to tell us, "I like the idea of a woman asking me for a date, but I'd lose interest if she did." They like the notion, but they don't like the reality. The same is true about being pursued after they've caught you. They might invite it, but if you actually do it, more often than not they will feel trapped and back off, or drop out.

• THE GOLDEN MEAN •

"A good relationship is based on mutual respect and a relatively equal balance of power," says Susan Forward, Ph.D., in her book (with Susan Torres) *Men Who Hate Women and the Women Who Love Them*. This is a fine idea, but in my experience the relatively equal balance of power is not always necessary or even desirable to maintain as a constant in a loving relationship.

The balance of power may shift. It may never be equal. There is nothing wrong with one person being more in control, if both partners agree that's what they want. The kind of person who is uncomfortable with power will seek out a stronger mate who will take on the responsibility, and relieve him or her of the need to take charge.

But go slowly if you decide to change the original equation and take back some power. Go about shifting the balance very carefully. The first danger is changing the rules without adequate warning and negotiation. Give change time. The second danger is waiting too long to leave if there isn't going to be any change. If the situation is no longer working for you, and there's no hope of making it different, get out and get on with your life. In our experience, take-charge men are not good bets for rehabilitation.

On the other hand, if you are the one who is being too controlling, try to make the conversion quickly. We have found that by the time a man is ready to admit to that vague feeling of being smothered, the relationship is on the way out. If you care, retool fast.

Redirect some of that domineering energy in other ways. Use your power to build self-esteem rather than to dominate your partner. Use it to enhance your life and his. If you are creative or adventurous, you may bring a different point of view to him. Your strength and knowledge can often be an inspiration. But *offer* it. Don't shove it down his throat.

If you can grow in your self-esteem, you can be more trusting and give the man in your life a chance to demonstrate his love without prompting from you. Banish questions like, "Do you love me?"

When you let go of your tendency to direct and script his life, you'll find you have a lot more time and energy for other things. Like just having fun together.

• Chapter 3 •

Money, Work, And
The New Math

People probably lie more about money—having it, not having it, wanting it, not wanting it—than any other subject, including sex. That's why we don't trust what men tell us money means to them. Most men say it means the ability to be flexible, or to have fun, or it means freedom. They don't like to admit it makes them feel powerful or gives them status or security. But it's important for us at The Godmothers to know how money fits into their value system and their ideas about marriage when we go to match them up with a date.

A man who needs a lot of money in the bank to feel secure is going to go bananas with a woman who needs to spend his money to feel loved. But prying these secrets out of men is not easy. They lie about it to their parents and children, their lovers and spouses. Their wives or the women they live with often don't know their net worth or even their income.

Both men and women tell us that at one time or another they have had a bank account they didn't tell their spouses about. Men don't tell their wives how much they've really spent on a set of golf clubs or a new car. But when they're dating, they might be more apt to inflate what they spend, instead of playing it down. They might also like to give the impression—as one man-about-town did—that they're just waiting to be old enough to start dipping into their trust fund. In the meantime, the man-about-town didn't mind living off the kindness of friends. In fact, he felt it was his duty. It took the friends a long time to separate myth from fact.

A man's attitude toward money, and what he actually does with it, may be one of his most closely held secrets. Fortunately, The Godmothers have learned how to interpret the signs that make it easier to unravel the mysteries of the male money mystique.

• THE ECONOMICS OF DESIRE •

One thing we have discovered is that there's nothing like money anxiety to dampen the libido. Who's anxious about money? Everyone is, whether they have it or not. If they don't have it, they want it. If they do have it, they're worried about losing it or about making more. This makes commitment even more nervous-making than ever, because marriage is a tremendous financial risk.

Women who are successful come to me and say they want a man whose income matches or is better than theirs, and whose future is secure. They're afraid to marry any other kind of man. They worry that if his earning power is minimal, or if his business fails, they will become the sole support of the family.

Men, on the other hand, come in two varieties. Either they want to be the protector and take care of a woman totally, or they want a woman who can contribute to the household income. But unless they are rolling in dough, men are running scared about what commitment costs. It's the American way to aspire to a second home, a second car, a color television set in every room. It's a huge responsibility.

Women, as well as men, want to know what they're getting moneywise. Before she gets involved, the average woman wants to find out what the guy is worth. But how does a woman discover his bottom line? He smiles and says, "I was brought up not to talk about money," or, "Don't trouble your pretty little head about money." The sixty-year-old wife of the owner of one of the most famous resorts in the world said, "I was married for forty years and had no idea what my husband's financial situation was. He left the dinner table when I asked about our assets."

So how's a girl to know whether she's getting involved with a millionaire or a con artist? You could start with his clothes and his job, and then work your way through his housing situation and his possessions. But a millionaire might wear blue jeans and old tweed jackets and drive four-wheel-drive vehicles, and the sharp operator might be disguised in Armani suits and crocodile shoes and drive a Rolls-Royce. Clothes and cars do not make a man.

One of the best stories I've heard about how appearances can be deceiving, was told by a friend who always seemed to get tied up with impoverished artists. Finally, she had attached herself to a dashing real estate developer, who was about to be divorced, who had an office that screamed Fortune 500, a country house in Connecticut, and a Porsche. He wore impeccably tailored suits and wined and dined her in the most expensive restaurants. At last, she thought, she had found true love with a rich man, something she and her mother had thought was impossible.

The truth was, though, that Prince Charming's firm owned his office, he was house-sitting the Connecticut estate for a friend, the Porsche was leased by his firm, the dinners were written off as a business expense, and he had found a tailor in Hong Kong who turned out imitation Saville Row suits for a song.

What A Woman Can Do:

If he's anxious about your earning potential, try to fill him in without actually spelling it out or bragging—and don't do it on the first date. Keep it casual and light. If your financial outlook isn't too bright, don't bring it up at all. By the time *he* brings it up, he might be too smitten to care.

As for getting a fix on *his* financial profile, it isn't good form to run a Dunn & Bradstreet on him. And you can't grill him. We at The Godmothers can ask probing questions that you, a date, can't and shouldn't. Lay back and pay attention to details. Observe his friends and remember the stories he tells about his past. Does everything make sense? Does he ever contradict himself, or do his friends have stories that don't agree with his? If you are suspicious, try to get information subtly from friends in the same business, but be careful that this doesn't backfire and get back to him. If you act interested in his work life, he will probably volunteer enough information over a period of time for you to get an accurate fix on him.

Do You Really Want to Marry a Millionaire?

When I lecture in places like Ohio, I notice that men with money make a lot of jokes about how easy it is to attract women: "I have no trouble getting all the women I want. I just open my wallet," they say. There's a lot of truth in jokes. Think about it. Have you ever seen an ugly woman get out of a Porsche? Or a beautiful blonde with an older man who's poor?

But men who have comfortable incomes can be under financial pressure, too. Walter, a

CEO with a large manufacturing company, said he didn't want to date women with children, but he didn't say why. I suspected that it might be because he was spending big bucks to support his ex-wife and four children, and was skittish about taking on an additional financial burden. I went through my files and made suggestions. Finally, I came to a woman I thought was perfect. She did have children, but she was one of the top producers of a well-known stock brokerage house. I acted on my hunch and told Walter that although this woman had children, she also had enough of her own money to support them. He thought a minute, and then decided she was worth a try.

Another iffy proposition is the guy who has it, but doesn't want to spend it. The tip-off for me is what he tells me about his former girlfriends or wives. "She sure liked to spend my money," or, "I never saw anyone who could run up bills like that." The theme of all his stories is that women are only after him for his money. Maybe some of them are, but more likely, he's just plain stingy. I try to explain to dates I line up for this type that he might be idiosyncratic in the money department, but not to judge too quickly until they evaluate the total package, and decide whether the guy's charm, intelligence, or whatever, compensate for his difficulty parting with money.

Then there's the big spender who wants to take care of the women in his life. This guy is definitely not chintzy. They are like the distinguished WASP, the owner of a trucking business, who said to me, "I don't care if a woman earns money or doesn't. I have enough for both of us." I call these men protectors. Sounds like something a lot of women could get used to. But wait. Is there a price to pay?

I know an international financier who loves to lavish gifts on his women, to take them to Gstaad for skiing and to St. Bart's for sunning. Some women fall right into the plan, until they find out that he expects them to be ready to leave at a moment's notice when his business beckons, to play hostess when he's entertaining, in effect to be prepared to give up their own lives to lead his. These are the men who want women as an ego prop. They are willing to pay for the masseuse and the clothes that will produce an expensive-looking woman as an accessory, so that their friends will know they have arrived, and their enemies will drop dead with envy.

Some women will gladly turn into a glamorous geisha at the drop of a diamond bracelet. But not every woman is ready to pay the price, if living with someone who pays all the bills means that he owns her. Women today don't have to play these roles if they don't want to. The "new math" means they can have their own money from their own jobs and buy their own fur coats. They have choices. They don't have to submerge themselves in a man's life and get their kicks from his successes. They can aspire to their own successes.

• WOMAN'S WORK •

Protectors are rare. Most men tell me they are interested in dating a woman who works. Harrison, an editor in his fifties, who recently divorced his second wife, was particularly insistent about a woman who does *something*. "My second wife didn't do anything, and she became cloyingly dependent. I hated it." He asked for a woman with a career and interests of her own. When I asked, "Do you mean a job or a career?" he thought a moment. "A *career*. I want her to be as engaged in what she's doing, as I am in what I'm doing."

Interestingly enough, many younger men in their twenties and thirties answer that question differently. Yes, they want a second income, so they want a woman who works. But, they want her to work at a job, not a career. "If it's a career," said one thirty-year-old marketing manager with a large company, "then not an all-encompassing one." "No killer MBAs," said a man who was an MBA himself.

A thirty-four-year-old sound engineer with his own business, who my interviewer described in her report as "very handsome and calm with a great smile and great eyes," said emphatically, "No yuppies." He didn't want a competitive go-getter. He wanted someone who would have time for him and put him first. He had been living with a woman who had been rising quickly through the ranks at an insurance company. As she was subjected to more stress in her job, she was less and less willing to be the one to make the sacrifices to keep the relationship together.

"If you're both working long hours, unless you have identical outside interests, you can't spend any time together," he said. "The relationship has got to suffer. When I wanted to go somewhere, she was always working late. She began to expect me to help solve her problems all the time. Who was I supposed to tell *my* problems to?"

Women have traditionally been the nurturers, the ones for cultivating the emotional climate of relationships. But that takes time, which is why so many of the men who come to me make a point of requesting a woman who will have time for them. They may not put it quite that way, but when they're saying they don't want a woman who's too wrapped up in her career, what they often mean is they don't want a woman who won't make them their number-one priority.

What A Woman Can Do:

Perhaps because boys are raised by their mothers to believe that they are the center of the universe, men grow up expecting they will be adored that way by all women. Maybe they saw their mothers catering to their fathers, and they want the women in their lives to treat them the same way. But no matter how a man arrived at this state of expectation, the question a woman has to answer is, is there some way to satisfy his attention needs without sabotaging her own work needs.

A woman who has her own business is a good bet for a man who wants a woman to conform to his schedule, because she can often make time for him in a way that a woman locked into a corporate structure cannot. But she might be extremely busy, too. A smart woman I know, who runs a string of successful retail stores, found out that it was easier than she thought to satisfy her husband's requests for attention. For instance, he wanted her to serve him dinner when he came home. She discovered by trial and error that she didn't have to actually *cook* dinner. The housekeeper cooked dinner, and when she got home, she zapped it in the microwave oven, put it on a plate, and served it to her husband on a pretty tray. As long as she actually *served* it to him, he was satisfied.

You might find that it's okay to bury yourself in work, as long as you make him a priority now and then. Paying attention doesn't really take much time. Are you really *there* when you're there? A lot of people don't know how to listen. Become aware of whether you are focusing or letting your thoughts wander. And don't forget how to be spontaneous. Every once in awhile ask him to lunch or drop everything to go to a movie with him. Make sure he knows you were overcome with this terrific urge to be with him.

• SHE EARNS MORE THAN HE •

Working is one thing, but a woman who earns more than a man, or has a higher status job, presents a serious problem. We're not just talking time, we're talking money and ego. Many men are pleased with their wives' success, only if it doesn't surpass their own. Philip Blumstein, Ph.D., and Pepper Schwartz, Ph.D., found in an exhaustive study they reported on in their book *American Couples*. As more women earn more money than men, "it will be unsettling to many men because money translates to power and men are unaccustomed to yielding power to women."

We all know men who handle this situation with aplomb: The secure man who's pleased with his girlfriend's success and finds it easy to live with or the man who's happy to find a woman who will support him while he writes the Great American Novel. And there have always been men who try to marry the boss's daughter or become the husband of someone famous.

A salary should not be a test of a person's worth. The amount of money someone earns should not be the critical factor in human interaction. But in an imperfect world, it still is. A lot of men and women can't handle a relationship where she earns more than he. It's too tough to buck tradition or a fragile ego to date a female partner in a law firm where you're still an associate, or to go out with a woman who's your boss.

Men tend to equate money and position with masculinity. They don't want to date women who earn more or have higher status jobs, because it makes them feel impotent and insignificant instead of powerful and important. They surrender a view of themselves they can't afford to lose.

Most men get on an ego trip from supporting women, in a way that most women don't share when the roles are reversed. In fact, many women are actively uncomfortable as the primary breadwinner.

Jan and Herb split up, he told me, because she didn't like making more money than he did. She did well selling real estate, and kept trying to convince him to join her. He was still hoping to make a go of a restaurant he ran with two partners. Jan kept telling him that her father had always supported her mother, and she expected Herb to support her so that she could stop working and have children. She nagged constantly. The pressure finally destroyed their sex life. Herb moved out.

Randolph was married to Veronica, who had inherited a nice piece of change from her grandfather. With wise investing, she parlayed her money into a tidy income. Randy, meanwhile, was struggling to keep first one business and then another afloat. Veronica lost no opportunity to lord it over Randy. She ordered him around in front of friends. She was deaf to his need for sympathy from her. He is a fair-minded, mild-mannered guy. He didn't want to struggle for attention and appreciation. He found another woman who gave it to him gladly.

What A Woman Can Do:

There's nothing inherently wrong with a woman having more money than a man. Nowhere is it written that that's a bad thing. The trouble starts with how men and women react to it. Does he feel relieved or emasculated? Does she feel gratified or taken advantage of? Does he pressure her or vice versa?

It doesn't help if a woman nags a man to make more money, or if she keeps putting him down. It's easier to control what you do than what he does. If you're the guilty one, and you care about making a relationship work, now's the time to get your act together.

When Veronica saw that she was going to lose Randy, she realized she loved him too much to give him up without a struggle. She went to a shrink who helped her to convert her considerable energy into changing herself into a more understanding and less demanding person. Randy went back to her because he really loved her, too. With Veronica on his side, bolstering his ego instead of tearing it down, he was able to turn his laboratory testing business around. He feels a lot better about himself, and Veronica can take some of the credit for that, too.

• WHO PAYS? •

Who pays when you go out on a date? You thought that was all settled. Well, it's not. There is still a lot of confusion and hostility surrounding the issue, because what men expect is not always what women expect.

A twenty-eight-year-old accountant told us that a woman he had just met asked him to dinner. They went to a fashionable restaurant and had a great dinner. He thought they were enjoying each other's company. When the bill came, he expected her to pick up the check.

When she didn't make a move, he said, "Why don't we split it down the middle?" She grew indignant. He said, "You asked me out, so the least you can do is pay your share." She stalked out of the restaurant.

Then there was the man who told us the way he reacts on a first date if a woman whips out her credit card and wants to split the bill. He says, "It tells me she just wants to be friends, or that she's a feminist. In either case, I'm not interested."

A woman I know said, "I tried to pay for dinner on the third date with a fifty-year-old banker. He laughed as I did it. I never heard from him again."

Confusing? There is often (but not always) a difference between how a twenty-nine-year-old and a forty-nine-year-old man will react to who pays, because of how things were done when they first started dating, or because of how much disposable income they have. Usually what we hear from younger men is that they expect women to share expenses in some way. When you're twenty-nine, it's too heavy a burden to pay the tab for two for dinners, concerts, dancing, time after time. "If she has a good job, she should pay for something once in a while, or ask me over for dinner and to watch a film on her VCR," says a twenty-seven-year-old client who works with a research and development firm. "We're both starting out. Women have great educations and jobs. It's not fair for one to pay all the time, especially if you're seeing each other on an ongoing basis."

But a lot of men are reluctant to tell this to a date. They might resent freeloading, yet they'd sooner drop the woman than bring up the subject. A lot of women don't know how to bring up the subject either. If they've been rebuffed for pulling out their wallet, they are doubly wary the next time.

What A Woman Can Do:

If splitting a check down the middle or paying your own way seems too businesslike and unromantic, there are other less abrasive ways to contribute, at least until you get to know him better. You can buy the theater or movie tickets, pack the picnic supper to take to the concert in the park, invite him to a charity benefit you've paid to attend. One couple I fixed up arranged a vacation together. He supplied free frequent flyer tickets to Europe, she paid for hotels, and they split everything else.

If he's over forty-five and/or wealthy, don't rush to pick up checks. But unless he's made it clear that he is paying for everything, the important thing is to keep up your end of things, without making a big deal of it. At the least, this approach will keep you out of trouble until you know him well enough either to understand his wishes or to ask him how he'd like you to handle your end of the expenses, whichever comes first.

• THE ROOT OF ALL EVIL •

As people get closer in a relationship, it becomes less who pays for what and more how the money is used. "It's the attitude toward money that's important," says a divorced client who is fifty-two. "If she's crazy about money, I'd be less attracted to her. A woman who's fixated on money is likely to be using it as a symbol for getting affection. You know, 'If you love me, buy me a diamond ring.' No thanks."

When you have two people with different values and attitudes, money becomes a flash point for conflict. She believes in paying bills right away. He doesn't mind owing money. He wants to invest income for the future. She thinks you should spend everything you make and live it up. Are you using money as a symbol for love, a power tool, an ego prop?

A couple I know met in a college in Vermont. Beth was an art major and Gordon was in the MBA program. When they graduated, they decided to stay together, but they began to have problems. She wanted to live in a small town; he wanted to move to the city. They settled on a smallish city in New England where he became involved in union negotiations, and she taught art.

At first they were frugal because money was scarce, but as Gordon earned more money and he was expected to travel in more affluent circles, he began to buy better clothes and entertain. He would have liked to do some of the business entertaining at home, but Beth didn't like to cook and she was a real klutz at entertaining. Gordon is willing to pay for a housekeeper and for caterers. He wants to buy Beth more stylish clothes, but she thinks all of this is too extravagant and resists. They fight all the time. How they want to spend money is a metaphor for how Beth and Gordon want to live, what is important to each of them.

It might not be easy to discover how the man in your life feels about money, but here are some questions that might help to clarify your own attitudes. After you've answered for yourself, use your intuition to figure out how *he* would respond. How do the two of you match up?

1. You see a friend buy a Mercedes. Do you feel jealous? Do you think it's an excessive expenditure? Would you like to go out with a man who owns a fancy car? Would you like to own one yourself?

2. When you travel, do you like to stay in the most luxurious and expensive hotels? At a bed and breakfast, or something in between?

3. If you inherited $100,000, would you find the bank with the best rate of interest? Buy high-risk stocks? Put it into a down payment for an apartment? Buy a fur coat? Throw parties for your friends?

4. A friend, who's the head buyer for her department in a specialty store, marries a man who teaches high school and will probably always make less money than she. Do you think she did the right thing? Would you do that?

5. You always pay bills right away? Save them until the end of the month and pay them at one time? Put off paying until the letters from the people you owe money become threatening?

6. You are dating a man who insists you pay your share. Would you stop dating him? Continue dating him but resent it? Cheerfully pay up?

7. Someone you've been dating is having a hard time financially. Will you pick up the tabs? Stop going to expensive places? Insist he pay his share?

8. If you're seeing a man who's making more money than you are, do you insist on contributing sometimes? Buy him presents? Let him spend it all because he has it?

9. When you meet a man, what do you think about first: His attitude toward relationships? What he does for a living? Whether he's a good conversationalist? How much money he makes? How he feels toward you, how he treats you, how interested is he in you?

• LOVE AND WORK •

Psychologists point out that when arguments over money become frequent in a relationship—where economic survival isn't at stake—the battle is really over other issues. All these skirmishes over who pays for what, who earns what, and how to spend money, are really about what money stands for.

Now that women can earn money, too, the equation has changed. Everyone has more choices. In our experience, a few men want to be caretakers, a few want to be taken care of, but most of them like the idea of sharing the responsibility, as long as the woman's contribution isn't too threatening.

Secretly, men are relieved to be able to combine love and money and not have to give up one for the other. This is when the economics of desire work for them and lessen the financial risk of an ongoing relationship or marriage. They can have their cake and eat it, too. Love *and* money.

• Chapter 4 •

Is There Sex After Dating?

Men are more secretive about sex than almost anything else—except money—at least with women. "You do it—you don't talk about it," grinned a twenty-eight-year-old client. Men may not discuss sex with women, but they certainly talk to each other about what they do and how they do it, in graphic detail.

One successful young realtor was bragging to a friend about his new ladylove. They were sitting side by side on a banquette in a busy restaurant, he said, when she suddenly unzipped his fly and grabbed him under the tablecloth. He was surprised and delighted. It was all so spontaneous. "Hmmm," his friend frowned. "It may have seemed spontaneous to you, but don't you think she's done it before?" That made the adventure seem less special, even sordid. The seed of doubt had been planted, but he couldn't bring himself to ask the woman in question whether or not she had ever committed such an act before in a restaurant. Instead, he just wondered and fretted.

I have found that men don't usually tell their sexual fantasies to women. They are surprised and delighted if a woman shares *her* fantasies, and they are tickled to act them out. With a lot of coaxing they might be persuaded to talk about their own. Sometimes they drop hints. If a man buys a woman lace panties or a black garter belt, chances are he likes dressing up for bed. But it'll probably be up to her to fill in the blanks to see just how far he'd like to go—and if he wants to join in the dressing fun, too.

The most serious problem women face, though, is that men don't always want to talk about love when they're preoccupied with sex. A guy thinks, "I don't know how I feel about this woman, except I know I want to go to bed with her." Men tell me that ideally they would put love and sex together, but they aren't too fastidious if it doesn't work out that way—they'll make do with what they have. This creates a dilemma for women who really want to hear the *L* word before they hit the sack with a guy—or at least have it introduced into the conversation not too long after.

• RECREATIONAL SEX •

Marta was excited about her blind date with Roger. One of her best friends had arranged it and built Roger up as a suave European and an up-and-coming producer in the venture capital firm where he worked. Marta, who was twenty-eight, had recently ended a long-term relationship, and was having trouble getting back into the swim of dating. She dressed carefully because they were going out to dinner at what she assumed would be a nice restaurant, and she used some of the new Poison perfume she had gotten for her birthday.

Roger lived up to his billing. He was thirty-four and looked and sounded like a young Charles Boyer. They went to a fashionable French restaurant that was too crowded and smokey for her taste, but where Roger was known and deferred to. He monopolized the conversation and didn't seem terribly interested in finding out anything about her. Marta mostly listened. Although he didn't talk about anything personal, his stories were amusing and the time passed pleasantly.

The restaurant was near where she lived so they walked home. For a moment she hesitated at the lobby door. Should she ask him up for coffee or a drink? It seemed like the polite thing to do since it was early and he had spent a lot of money on dinner. But no sooner did they settle on the sofa with cognac than he was all over her. "Now wait a minute," Marta laughed. "Hold on." He couldn't be serious.

"But I don't want to hold on," Roger said. "I want to go to bed with you."

He was serious. There had been no buildup, not even any flirting. Marta was flabbergasted, but she didn't want to hurt his feelings. "I'd like to get to know you better before I go to bed with you," she said.

"What better way to get to know someone than in bed?" Roger countered.

Marta was courteous but firm. She had no desire to go to bed with Roger. She was attracted to him, but she didn't even *know* him. She would have liked to get to know him, and then maybe that would have been in the cards, but he didn't want to talk about it. He got sulky, almost nasty. She had blown it. It was obvious that she would never see him again.

For Marta and many other women, the idea of casual affairs has become depressing, not to mention dangerous because of AIDS. In their early twenties many women may want to go to bed with every man they meet, but as they approach their thirties they are looking for a deeper relationship. The idea of the "zipless fuck" has lost its charm. They have learned that more sex partners doesn't necessarily mean better sex. Anyone who's recently divorced, of course, after spending her twenties with the wrong man, might go for some experimentation.

Even in the age of AIDS, most men have no compunction about falling into bed with an available woman who seems reasonably safe. In fact, they feel as if they are *owed* sex when they date a woman. One attractive financial consultant told me, "I don't have time to waste if it's not going to work out. I'll wait for three or four dates, but why should I spend my time and money on a woman if it's not going to lead anywhere?"

When I ask men of all ages how they feel about sex without love, they have no problem. "Sex without love is easy," says a forty-nine-year-old man. "It's fine," says a thirty-two-year-old, "but the thrill is greater with feelings." Many prefer sex and emotion combined, it's true, but they won't stand on ceremony. They might, however, go through the motions of pretending to be in love, just to create the illusion of passion a woman wants, if that seems like the expedient thing to do. "Actually," one man explained, "at that moment, I believe it myself."

It's not uncommon for women to opt for casual sex on occasion, but I've never heard of a woman faking love. Orgasm, yes—but being in love, no. One of the great unspoken differences between men and women, in my experience, is that probably more women are less inclined to settle for anything less than the real thing. For men it's wasting time *not* to go to bed. For women it's wasting time to go to bed *with the wrong man.*

• VIVE LA DIFFERENCE •

Women always report that they have better sex if there's an emotional component. One reason is that men and women are aroused by different stimuli. Men react more to visuals than women. They are often quite explicit about what they want: One man ordered women with straight brown hair and girlish figures; another wouldn't go out with anything but bosomy blondes. Some insist on tall, others on short. One man we know, who was seeing a willowy blond WASP, said he kept fantasizing his ideal dark-haired gypsy every time he made love to her. She fitted into his lifestyle and was perfect in every other way, but he finally left her.

Women are sometimes attracted to a particular body type, but they are much more flexible. Visual images play a much larger role in male fantasy life. Men start with turn-on magazines when they are boys, and the right package never seems to lose that ability to turn them on.

Women have never been known to react in the same way to male pinups. Typically, a woman needs a combination of stimuli—visual, tactile, and emotional—to get turned on. This is one explanation for why sex with a stranger is often disappointing for women. A close encounter with a good-looking hunk without the right emotional component just isn't the big thrill it seemed it would be. Even the novelty isn't necessarily a turn on.

Men tell me that they are excited by variety, by someone new. As one man in his thirties put it, "My interest in a woman diminishes after I've had sex with her a number of times. There's adventure in a new woman." Variety seems to continue to titillate men of all ages. Nothing beats the ego boost of a new conquest.

This causes some discouraging conflicts of interest. He's not going to go public with it, but the greatest fear of many men is sexual failure, so they try to bolster themselves with the proof of their virility and seductiveness. The major fear of most women is not being loved. That's why it's more important for women to cultivate an ongoing, caring relationship with one person. Sex is an avenue to closeness and intimacy for women. Not only does closeness and intimacy give her better sex, it gives her the love she wants. Recreational sex is okay in its place, but it's not a big deal.

Unfortunately, something else is going on in the psyche of men. Not only does frequent recreational sex give them the illusion of omnipotency, it also banishes threatening feelings of dependency and vulnerability. One of our clients in his mid-forties, who was always afraid of being rejected, told me that he used to treat sex as a game because then it was easier for him to withdraw. He realized how unrewarding that had been, and he said he is now working hard at developing emotionally connected relationships.

What A Woman Can Do:

Look for partners who are in the same stage of evolution as you are. If you are trying to find closeness, you are going to be mighty disappointed with a fun-and-games man. Every woman gets swept off her feet once in a while, so don't worry if that happens. It's not terminal. Just move on if he's not on your wavelength.

• DAMNED IF YOU DO, DAMNED IF YOU DON'T •

One of the questions I'm most often asked by women is, "When should I go to bed with him?" In some circles there's an unwritten rule that you sleep with a man on the third date. I am not a believer in that law, or any other. Younger men feel some urgency about bedding dates. Others, especially middle-aged men, take it slower. These are the men who are more apt to feel an obligation to continue a relationship once they've initiated sex.

I've heard men say that they'd like to go to bed with women on the first date. "I wouldn't go out with a woman I didn't want to go to sleep with," a forty-year-old divorced man told me. "After the first encounter, I'm either attracted to her or I'm not, in which case I wouldn't date her again. But I can wait, if I think there's some point to it. I don't push if I'm interested."

Some men, on the other hand, don't care about having sex with every woman they date. They can't summon up the energy or the libido. All those older men you see in smart places with young chicks are not necessarily bedding them down every night. Some have confessed to me that the fantasy is sufficient. Besides, they're too tired after a night on the town to hazard the real thing.

Men have different ways of auditioning new prospects. One thirty-eight-year-old biochemist with a very structured life arranges drink dates. Then he has his secretary beep him at a prearranged time so he can have an out if he wants one, or a way of ending the preliminary interview. This way he doesn't spend any more time than he has to with an unpromising prospect.

I never realized how important first impressions are for both sexes, until we at The Godmothers conducted a survey we called The Ten-Minute Study. Almost 90% of the men and women we studied entertained two out of three of the following thoughts, within the first ten minutes of meeting: "Would I want to see this person again?" "Sleep with the person?" "Marry the person?" The opinions formed in those opening minutes never changed.

Today the assumption is that a date is available for sex, if the conditions are right, but there's no way of knowing what other commitments a person has. It's reasonable to take it for granted that the person is single, but we all know of cases where that wasn't so. An even riskier assumption is that a person isn't dating anyone else.

I know a forty-seven-year-old divorced owner of a major corporation who flies his own plane and cruises the Caribbean in his own sailboat. After breaking up with his last long-term relationship, he started having a sexual relationship with his secretary. But she isn't up to his standards for a companion, so he's dating a number of other women in his search for a steady replacement. Since he doesn't want to keep three or four sexual relationships going at the same time, his only sex partner is the secretary. That's good because at least the man has a sense of responsibility. But it's also bad because for him sex is only a job description and doesn't demand loyalty.

What A Woman Can Do:

How do you know how serious a man is, or whether he's even actually available for a relationship? Many men expect sex early in the dating cycle. If you refuse, he may not call again. But you may give in before you're ready or know his intentions, and he might just be looking for a quickie. He might say, "Don't have any expectations," as one charmer did that we heard about—after the act had been consummated.

Sex is not a surefire way to attract a man. Remember that you don't have to give in to instant demands. If you want to wait until you're sure the feelings are mutual, stand your ground. To paraphrase the old chestnut, "I wouldn't want to belong to any club that would have me as a member," "I wouldn't want to have sex with anyone who would want me to do it without caring about him."

• PASSION AND AGGRESSION •

Rupert was a banker whose wife had left him for a starving artist. He was a real catch. Every woman in town was after him, so Cynthia was delighted when mutual friends asked her to join them for dinner one night. She was even more delighted when Rupert called her several days in advance and said, "Let's meet before this dinner because it's going to be awkward getting to know each other with other people around." They went out for drinks which extended into dinner and a nightcap. There was definitely electricity between them. The night they were supposed to be meeting for the first time, they kept their delicious secret about already knowing each other to themselves. When they were finally alone, they both dissolved with laughter.

They had gotten so close so quickly that Cynthia welcomed Rupert's invitation to come up to see his apartment. It seemed inevitable that they would quickly be in each other's arms on the sofa. There they remained for what seemed to Cynthia like an eternity. She was wrinkling her new silk dress and felt inhibited by all those clothes they were wearing. Finally she said, "Wouldn't we be more comfortable in the bedroom?" After all, they weren't adolescents who had to spend so much time necking. They were adults who could get down to real business.

Rupert led her into the bedroom and they silently took off their clothes. The passionate kissing began again, but now something was wrong. Rupert wasn't responding. No matter what he tried, and what Cynthia tried, the hardness he had experienced on the sofa had vanished. He couldn't get it up. "This has never happened to me before," he said. Cynthia cooed sympathetically and put her clothes back on. Rupert was irreparably embarrassed. Even though he said he'd call her, Cynthia feared the worst, and it came to pass. She never heard from him again. She blamed herself for being too aggressive. The poor guy had just had a humiliating rejection from his wife, had little practice or recent experience with new women, and here she'd put him on the spot before he was ready to perform.

Even though they hate to admit it, many men do suffer from performance anxiety. They worry about being good lovers, about "doing it" right. Rupert needed more time. When Cynthia was so explicit about what she wanted, he became intimidated. Cynthia realized, after the fact, that she should have let Rupert take the lead, that in his fragile condition he needed to set the pace. She seemed so powerful and free. He wasn't sure he could live up to her expectations.

Do men want women to be sexually aggressive? Gay Talese, who wrote a book about sex in America called *Thy Neighbor's Wife*, said in an interview that a lot of men are passive and need help. They would welcome women initiating sex, and also taking charge of their own sexual fulfillment. The Woody Allens of this world, who seem scared and nervous about sex, appeal to the maternal instincts of women. Their anxiety brings out the desire to be helpful and protective. Some of these guys look like they'd never get anywhere if some kind woman didn't take over. All the men I've asked, "How do you feel about women making the first move?" answer that they like the idea of women initiating sex. However, I tend not to believe this. I go with the caveat that one man offered, "part of me would love it, but there are still elements of social taboo about it."

What A Woman Can Do:

Sexual aggression is tricky. True, many men today are not threatened by a confident, uninhibited woman, but just how aggressive is aggressive? Too much aggression can be a turnoff. It can arouse anxiety rather than lust. A man won't usually tell a woman to slow down, that he needs to move at a slower pace. He won't say, "You seem so confident that I'm worried about whether I can live up to your expectations." This is dangerous territory, so go into it forewarned.

• HOLDING BACK •

The other extreme is a woman who is too shy. A certain amount of hesitation can be appealing and reassuring to a man. A man who is sexually reticent himself might be relieved to move at a slower pace. But as the relationship grows, persistent shyness can limit sexual sharing. As two people get to know and trust each other better, defenses should crumble and reticence disappear. Men like to know that a woman is enjoying herself in bed, too. When she telegraphs her pleasure, he gets an extra charge.

As an affair or marriage progresses, and sex gets boring and perfunctory, it usually spells trouble. One or both partners is going to go looking for a change. This is when men start searching for a younger and more enthusiastic alternative. When we asked our male clients whether a woman's aptitude for sex influenced their decision about whether to pursue a relationship, they said, "Sure." As one writer put it, "It's not the whole reason for seeing someone, but it's an important one."

Another man said, "Sexual behavior reflects how people feel about each other. Technique is overrated, but how a person behaves in bed reflects what they're like. You can't tell after one time in bed, but eventually it comes out."

Are *you* holding back too much? Do you ever:

1. Make the first move after the third or fourth date?
2. Take a shower or bath together?
3. Keep the lights on during sex?
4. Tell him what feels good?

5. Watch him when he climaxes?
6. Suggest new positions?
7. Suggest new locations to make love?
8. Let yourself go vocally?
9. Discuss your fantasies—and his? (Remember, you don't have to go along with his suggestions, if they're too far out for you.)
10. Try to seduce him?
11. Talk about lovemaking afterward?

What A Woman Can Do:

You've just met him and you're not sure what he likes. You can't go wrong with holding back and following his cues. You are progressing very nicely with the affair and feel comfortable with him in bed. This is the time to experiment with initiating sex or with being more explicit about what you want in bed. Try a little playfulness, seduction, abandon. You sense that he's getting bored with your routine. Why not create some suspense and intrigue? Try to introduce space and even tension to make him feel he has to win you all over again.

Men may be ambivalent about whether they want women to initiate sex, but not about wanting women to participate.

How to be Sexier

1. Try to be more spontaneous and unpredictable.

2. Let him know how much you are enjoying sex.
3. Work on enhancing your own body image.
   If you feel good about your body, he will,
   too.
4. You don't have to be in control all the
   time, especially not in bed where being
   out of control is a plus.
5. Aim for sex time when you are both relaxed and not worried about a 7:00 A.M.
   appointment. Banish beepers from the
   bedroom.
6. Find out what he likes, and tell him what
   you like.

• THE BIG PICTURE •

Joe had known Carly for six months. They
had fallen into a routine of dating once during
the week and then on weekends. For awhile
they always had sex when they had a date. One
night Joe just didn't feel like doing what was
expected of him, so he begged off and went
home. He knew Carly was a little perplexed,
but he wasn't prepared for the kind of pressure he felt from her after their next date.
They cuddled awhile, but he could feel how
tense she was. It really turned him off. The
more she continued to press, the more he continued to withhold.

We use sex as a metaphor for many emotions—love, fear, jealousy, revenge. Joe didn't
even know that he was trying to get back at

Carly because she had become too demanding in other areas of their relationship. It wasn't until she took a step back that she realized she had to ease up, not only her demands for sex, but on the other pressure she was exerting on him to show up on time, to call her more often, to share more of his thoughts and emotions with her. When she realized he would only give her what she wanted when he felt it was his own idea, Carly let up with the constant demands. She didn't have to say a word about it. Joe was sensitive enough to pick up the new vibes, and to respond to them quickly. Their lovemaking was never better.

Being angry can ruin your sex life. Resentment about other aspects of their life can turn a couple's bedroom into a battlefield, or—just as bad—into a boring place to be. People use sex to satisfy their needs and emotions. They use it for reassurance and solace. They use it as a lure and a weapon. If one or the other partner has a pattern of unreasonably withholding sex, of persistent impotence or frigidity, or lack of sexual interest, it might be because of other unresolved problems. A woman who wants more love might feel turned off by sex unless she gets more attention. A man who needs to be in charge might "punish" his partner by being insensitive to her needs.

What A Woman Can Do:

If the battle between the sexes is raging in your bedroom, it's time to declare a truce.

This is one place where feelings and preferences need to be openly discussed. The person in control doesn't necessarily win. If one partner isn't caring and concerned about the feelings of the other, they could *both* lose, because the experience will fall short of what it could be.

A sex problem could be a symptom of other problems in the relationship. If he won't talk about it, and you can't figure out what to do, consider the help of a sex therapist or counselor. A professional might have more success getting him to open up.

• WILL IT LAST? •

When will familiarity start to dull the shine on the sexual relationship? Men admit to liking variety and newness, but that doesn't mean they always act on it. Inertia is also at play, although they wouldn't like to admit *that*. But this is one of the persistent dilemmas of dating. If I start to go to bed with him too soon, will he tire of me sooner? If I don't start to go to bed with him when he's ready, will he go away and find another partner? Or, try this one on for size, how can I keep him interested after the first excitement wears off? After we do it on the porch swing, then what?

I tell women that being realistic is the best weapon. Men like variety, so why not be exciting and fresh in bed and out? You don't have to resort to Marabel Morgan tactics and show up at the front door dressed in Saran Wrap and cowboy boots, but life can be more fun for everyone if you act out fantasies, encourage playfulness, create romantic scenarios. Men like to pursue, so why not let yourself be pursued once in a while. In other words, forewarned is forearmed. Scope out the guy of your dreams, and play up to his weaknesses. It's all fair.

• Chapter 5 •

The Age of AIDS

Among the men who come into my office (all straight, incidentally), some are panicked about AIDS and some could care less, but they all play it low-keyed with women. I might get a third degree about a prospective date's background, but they're Joe Casual in person.

Although acquired immune deficiency syndrome (AIDS) was identified in 1981, it took quite a few years for heterosexuals to recognize that AIDS wasn't just a plague visited on homosexuals. But people caught on quickly when it became clear that the AIDS virus had begun infecting the general public.

As of this writing, there are an estimated 1.5 to 2 million Americans who are infected with the human immunodeficiency virus (HIV), which can cause AIDS. Not all HIV carriers will develop AIDS themselves, but they can transmit it to others who could develop AIDS. In other words, you don't have to have AIDS to give it to another person. People with HIV will be carriers for life, unless a way of destroying the virus is discovered. Intravenous drug users and prostitutes are already spreading the virus among the straight community. Women who have had sexual relations with bisexual men, or who have contracted the virus from contaminated blood, are passing it on to their babies and other lovers. Suddenly, everyone is suspect.

Some men tell me that the AIDS epidemic hasn't changed their attitudes toward sex or the women they get involved with. Others are actually relieved that they can get off the fast sex track. For men who like to take their time about falling into bed, concern about AIDS is a convenient excuse. Men with performance anxiety say it's relaxing to flirt, knowing that nothing will have to happen.

But the changes are real and legitimate. Caution and distrust crop up in the most unlikely places. You can see it in the way romance evolves in the movies and in soap operas on television. You can hear it in rock lyrics. In an era when sex and danger are linked, it's not so cool to brag about making love to a million girls. The shy guy is in, Casanova is out. Pop songs are extolling the virtues of monogamy and marriage. Fooling around might just be too dangerous.

• THE NEW IDEAL WOMAN •

In the first James Bond movie after heterosexual AIDS consciousness had been raised,

The Living Daylights, Bond confined himself to one woman, instead of his usual three, and instead of being the usual silly bimbo, the object of his attentions is an intelligent and talented cellist. What's going on here? I think it's the same thing I hear when a man tells me, "I tend to slum less than I used to."

Men are beginning to think, what types are the riskiest? A girl who goes disco dancing every night or a model who has an active sex life isn't the safest choice. Someone who was free with her sexual favors would have been ideal in the pre-AIDS era, but frankly, she's suspect right now. I find that men are skittish about the party girl type. They don't put it into so many words. Instead men are telling us that they want someone "serious." Of course she has to have a sense of humor. What they mean is they want a solid citizen type, someone to take home to introduce to Mom and Dad or to their children. Someone responsible and dependable is not only more likely to have a clean bill of health, she is also more likely to stay faithful in the future.

What A Woman Can Do:

It is obvious that this is not the time to boast about your past conquests. It never was a good idea, but that kind of talk has taken on new significance. This is the time to boast about your innocence. If that doesn't wash, just stay off the subject altogether.

Also, at the same time that men are looking

for women who are less of a threat, women should be conscious of the kind of men who aren't good sex risks. The same rules apply: Men who've had multiple sex partners, who might continue to play the field, or who aren't "serious," have high risk potential.

• SCREENING THE CANDIDATES •

Since the AIDS virus stays in a person's system forever, someone who contracted it five years ago and doesn't have any symptoms can still be a walking time bomb. A person's past history has become just as important as his or her present. One of our clients in his forties says, "I'm much more cautious and careful." He says he spends more time talking to women about their past than he used to. "There are a lot of women who used to sleep with gays to reform them." The women he meets are more apt to have done that than to have slept with intravenous drug users (another high risk group) or to be intravenous drug users themselves. He doesn't tell them his concerns or ask them flat out whether they've ever had gay lovers. But if something doesn't feel right to him, and if he has unresolved doubts, he just passes on to the next prospect.

Another man told us, "I'm less likely to fall in bed with someone I met at a party than I would have before." He, too, tries to get a history of past relationships and past drug use.

But short of cross-examination, all of the

questions you can think of to ask won't necessarily get to the heart of the matter. And even if they did, how would you know whether the answer you get is the truth. As one woman said in an interview in the New York *Post*, "I try to screen the new men in my life. I ask them questions, but how can you believe them? Men will say anything to get laid."

The answer for both men and women is to spend time getting to know a person, their background, friends, idiosyncracies, before taking them on as a sexual partner. As you get more intimate, more past history will be revealed than would ever be under direct questioning. Dr. Helen Singer Kaplan, author of *Women and AIDS: How to Eliminate the Risks Without Giving up Love and Sex*, says, "If you take out your notebook and demand to know how many women he's slept with, you don't have to worry about AIDS, because he's not going to stick around."

Even if you glean your facts in the most subtle, caring way, important information can be overlooked. One poignant story revolves around a woman in Philadelphia who contracted HIV from her long-time lover. He had gotten HIV from a blood transfusion and didn't know he was a carrier. He subsequently developed AIDS and died. She was still waiting to see what her fate would be.

Getting to know a person better is helpful, but admittedly imperfect. What are the other choices? Right now they are abstinence, testing, safer sex practices, and monogamy.

• ABSTINENCE •

The decision not to have sex is certainly a viable alternative. I know homosexuals who have eliminated sexual contact from their lives. They have seen enough of their friends sicken and die to want to swear off exposure to the same fate. They are not in a committed monogamous relationship and don't know where to turn that will be safe.

I hear about more and more heterosexuals who swear by abstinence, too. The new guy you meet might postpone sex for a long time without explaining why. Don't be surprised if he's committed to abstaining from sex until he gets married. The American Government and the Catholic Church support that position, and it makes sense for anyone who can't morally subscribe to any of the other alternatives or who is so panicked by the risk of AIDS that sex becomes distasteful. Suspicion can be a downer in the bedroom. If you're taking your fears to bed with you, your performance is sure to suffer.

But abstinence doesn't have to mean total deprivation. Dr. Helen Singer Kaplan and other sex therapists offer another way to make abstinence more bearable: masturbation. As Dr. Singer says, "No one will ever get AIDS from masturbation. It's the safest sex of all." The Kinsey Report in the fifties announced to the world that most people, even married ones, masturbate. Feminists welcomed it as an outlet that gave women a degree of independence. Men have always been more accepting of masturbation. Although studies since then have reported an increase in the number of women who masturbate, it is still a difficult subject for many of them to confront. With the AIDS epidemic, though, women who are going to opt for abstinence are going to discover that there is a way to take the edge off their desperation for a man until it feels right to take a chance again.

• TESTING •

Among the sexually active, testing has become a watchword. More and more articles have appeared by men and women who have voluntarily been tested. They invariably start out by saying that they are terrified of AIDS. As far as they are concerned, *everyone* is suspect. At least by being tested, they could determine whether they personally had HIV. Invariably, too, these writers have been in a low risk category. They had no symptoms of the disease and no reason to think they'd been exposed to it. Had their chances of harboring HIV been higher, would they have been as willing to be tested? We will never know, but they were motivated by the desire to lay to rest their own doubts. In each case, they are tremendously relieved and happy to be able to tell potential sex partners that they are HIV-free.

Testing may be a more universal answer some day when *everyone* is routinely checked for HIV, and checked every six months. One problem with AIDS testing is that it takes from three to six months for the antibodies of the virus to show up. You can get a clean bill of health and still be infected. The recommended procedure is to get tested, abstain for six months, and then get tested again to eliminate the possibility that the first test was too soon after contact with the infection.

But most of the people I talk to worry about another problem. How do you know whether or not you are courting disaster unless the *other person* has also been tested? "I'm not worried about whether I have it," a client told us. "I'm sure I'm okay. I'm worried about whether *she* has it." The number of people who are being routinely tested on a voluntary basis is so minuscule at this writing, that the lonely few with testing credentials are having a hard time finding each other.

One more chilling thought—even those who are tested don't always confess that they're carriers. A recent study in Chicago revealed that about one-fourth of a group of sexually active people taking tests for the AIDS virus told researchers that even if infection was confirmed, they would not warn casual sex partners. Maybe testing is the only sure way to determine who is a safe sex partner and who isn't, but if you can't depend on your potential lover to tell the truth about his or her test status, you're back to square one. Sex therapists William Masters and Virginia Johnson recommend that a couple be tested together and that the test results be sent to both or discussed in person with both present. Then you still have to trust your partner to be monogamous ever after to avoid future infection.

One more word of caution: there are men out there carrying bogus "certified AIDS-free" ID cards. Some of them don't know they're flashing a fake card. They have had blood drawn and paid for testing that was never done. But others never even tried to have a test. They just bought a card. They might joke about their golden AIDS-free card to their men friends, but you can count on them keeping the joke to themselves in front of women.

• SAFER SEX •

For those who have decided to remain sexually active, public health officials, doctors, and educators unanimously endorse safer sex practices. This can mean everything from stopping short of penetration to mutual masturbation. It usually means using a condom for vaginal or anal sex or fellatio and a dental dam (or improvised shield of plastic wrap) for cunnilingus. Since condoms never were foolproof when it came to birth control, there's no reason to believe they'll be foolproof when it comes to foiling the AIDS virus. No one knows for sure, but some researchers think the failure rate could be as high as 20% a year. Presumably dental dams and plastic wrap can fail, too. That's why authorities caution against a sense of false security when you are using prophylactics. There is no such thing as *safe* sex. Only *safer* sex.

There are ways, however, to get the best results from condoms:

1. Be sure it is made of latex, which is the most effective in blocking the AIDS virus. So-called natural condoms, made of lambs' intestines, may contain microscopic holes through which the virus can escape.

2. Latex deteriorates quickly when exposed to heat or light. That condom he's been carrying around in his wallet for the last year is definitely suspect.

3. Oil-based lubricants, such as petroleum jelly, also cause latex to deteriorate. Use a water-based lubricant such as K-Y jelly.

4. Obey the following rules when putting on a condom: Squeeze the tip of the condom to make sure there is no air in it and to leave room for the semen. Hold onto the tip while unrolling the condom carefully over the head and down the shaft of the erect penis. Make sure to unroll it all the way down to the hair at the base of the penis.

5. After orgasm, the condom must be

grasped at the base and held firmly during withdrawal to avoid spilling or leaking. It should be discarded at once.

Women need to know the nitty gritty details about condoms, because they buy at least 40% of all condoms and will probably buy more in the future. Packages designed to appeal to women feature pictures of couples hand-in-hand. Manufacturers are producing handy plastic pursepacks and special gold- or silver-plated condom cases for a touch of class. Condoms are positioned in vending machines at student unions and bars and at checkout counters where women will spot them.

Buying is one thing, but how do you get a guy to wear a condom? Women trade stories about how to do it. Men hate condoms. They always have and probably always will. They complain that it's like wearing a raincoat in the shower, that they lose their erections when they have to put them on, that it takes the intimacy out of the sex act.

Some of the more enlightened men tell me that they are resigned to having to use condoms, or they'll go along with it at first because they figure a woman will let them stop using a condom when she gets to know them better. "People make a big deal about it," said a thirty-year-old art director we know. "But we're adults now with a sense of humor. It's not like you're still an adolescent and worried and nervous about just going to bed with a girl. You've had experience and you can both be relaxed and laugh about it."

But more often it's the woman who takes the responsibility for safer sex. In an episode of a nighttime soap opera, after some steamy necking in the living room, the young heroine said, "Let's go into the bedroom. There are condoms in the bed table. I'll join you in a minute." In a popular movie, the heroine pops a packaged condom in her handbag before going out on a date with a man she's attracted to. Then she's embarrassed when someone else almost finds it. The message is clear. If you want a degree of protection, you'll have to rely on supplying the condom, even though that might be uncomfortable at times. Furthermore, women are finding they might have to manipulate, cajole, or trick their man into using it.

What A Woman Can Do:

Instant condom etiquette is evolving on the spot. Most women are making it up as they go along. Many have realized that it is up to them to educate their lovers on wearing condoms. Men are no longer shocked if women bring up the subject of using condoms, or if they even provide them. Just as men accepted the right of women to take charge of birth control, they are becoming used to them assuming the responsibility for safer sex.

Getting men to wear condoms is another matter. Some women have luck putting the condom on for the guy and making it a sexy part of foreplay. If you think your lover is going to be resistant, the best technique is probably to produce the condom at the moment it will be needed rather than to have a long and possibly argumentative discussion in advance—which isn't exactly the recommended prelude to a romantic interlude. But stick to your guns. Just remember that all over America other women are coping with the same problem. You are doing the right thing, and you are not alone.

• THE NEW MONOGAMY •

One-night stands are out. More sexual conservatism is in. Married couples are sticking closer to their legal mates and abandoning the game of musical marital chairs that was so popular in the seventies and early eighties. Most married men and women think twice about a quick sex fix. They are working at trying to improve their sex life within a marriage. Sex therapists report that their business has increased. More couples are coming in for premarital therapy, and miracle of miracles, increasingly men are the ones initiating the therapy. Couples are seriously committed to making sex work within their marriages or relationships. "Freelancing is just too risky," said a married man in his forties who used to "play around on the side."

Singles are taking more time to get to know their partners before jumping into bed. The people I see are definitely less interested in casual encounters than they ever were. The bloom is off the dating rose. They want to find the right person and see them exclusively.

Reports from college campuses confirm that trend. Everyone seems to be going steady. "Pinning" is back in style at fraternity houses. Some students are angry that they've been cheated out of their time of sexual freedom, that the sexual revolution is something they're going to hear about from their parents or read about in their history books. But the freedom of choice has been taken out of their hands. Fear of AIDS has encouraged the kind of caution that is reminiscent of the fifties. In fact, it's even more extreme. Students report that instead of going after a girl with a reputation for sleeping around, you stay as far away from her as possible.

One young Wall Street broker summed it up in a newspaper interview when he said, "It sounds cynical, but in a way, it's nice, easier to tie yourself down. There might be lots of fish in the sea, but they could all be poisoned, so who wants to go fishing?"

• THE AIDS GENERATION •

There are still men and women who have been unaffected by AIDS consciousness, let alone AIDS hysteria. But single heterosexuals, in particular, are waking up to the realities of the disease and trying to act more responsibly. At the very least, they are making an effort to get to know their sex partners better before going to bed with them. At the furthest extreme, they are abstaining from sexual contact altogether.

The people who come to me are usually quite rational in their approach. Men realize they have to be more cautious and discriminating. They might not *like* wearing condoms, but they know it's the responsible adult thing to do. They know sexual exclusivity is a reasonable alternative to the risk of playing the field—and they're even getting used to the idea. But the bottom line is trust. Trust has never been more important in relationships. Fraternity pins and wedding rings are significant symbols of fidelity, AIDS test results are concrete evidence of medical status, but what doesn't show or is not revealed is equally significant. And that you have to take on trust.

If it sounds as if sex and love are being reduced to a sensible and tame formula, never fear. Passion and romance are still alive and well. Although men may not talk about it openly, we still have incurable optimists coming to us who know that passion is irrational and messy, but who will take a chance on romantic love because they still believe that love will conquer all.

• Chapter 6 •

The Big C: Commitment

In the age of post-sexual liberation, many people have tired of the swinging singles lifestyle of singles' bars and bed hopping. They've had an attack of terminal boredom. They are afraid of herpes and AIDS. Monogamy and child-rearing never looked so good. Even marriage has come out of the closet. The men and women who come to me want to connect with a person who will enhance their lives, and then they want to settle in. They want to make a commitment. Men are often slower and more ambivalent than women, but in the end the majority want a committed relationship.

But what is a committed relationship? Commitment means mutual loyalty, trust, and love, but not necessarily permanence. Both men and women are often still torn between freedom and safety, between independence and marriage. These days women don't have to marry to buy security. They don't even have to marry to have children. Men don't have to marry to have a sexual partner. And yet both men and women are usually looking for a sexually exclusive and mutually satisfying arrangement, but that doesn't mean it has to have a marriage contract attached.

So if all these men say they want some kind of commitment, why does it seem that women are always the ones who are pushing for a committed relationship, and men are the ones who are trying to wriggle out of it? You know the story: A man knocks himself out getting the woman, then once he gets her, the woman knocks herself out to get him to make a commitment. The reason is that in spite of everything they say to women, many men are too scared to take that step.

• FEAR OF COMMITMENT •

In the second half of the eighties, the *New York Times Magazine* ran an article called "Why Wed? The Ambivalent American Bachelor." The author traveled around the country talking to men who were from thirty to forty-five years old. The latest U.S. Census Bureau report had told him that "not since the Great Depression had there been such a high proportion of bachelors in this age bracket." Why weren't they married at an age when their fathers had been raising kids and trying to save enough money for a larger house in the suburbs? What he found out was that they were "scared stiff" of getting married. Women in their thirties and forties are ready to marry or remarry and get on with domesticity, but why not these guys?

They know it would be good for them, but marriage is the great unknown. I call these men Professional Singles. They have made a career of being the extra man at dinner parties and of being introduced to every new girl on the block. They always find an abundant supply of compliant substitute wives to squeeze their orange juice. They have gotten so used to their single perks and they are so comfortable, that in spite of what they tell you and me about how much they want to find the right girl, I know when I see one of them that it's going to take more than that to make them give up their singlehood.

Part of the problem is age disynchronization. Men in their twenties want to get married, but women in their twenties often want to get a career established first. Then by the time the women turn thirty and decide it's time to think of husbands and babies, men of that age have gotten so used to bachelorhood and so skittish, that they don't know what they want. Besides, by this time they have become addicted to younger women, the ones in their twenties who are avoiding marriage for the time being.

The men in the above article regarded their singleness as a problem, and said they were afraid they might never marry. Yet their fear of "entrapment" was even higher. Women in that age group tend to be more anxious about *not* getting married. They constantly want reassurance about the status of a relationship. How is it going? Is it leading somewhere? By contrast, men seem cautious. They don't have the same urgency about finalizing arrangements. They are more apt to let matters drift. How often I have heard men say, "Our relationship was going just fine, but she was always pressing for another level of commitment."

Men are masters of indecision. As far as they're concerned, "If it ain't broke, don't fix it." If they think everything's going along all right, why stir things? "Yes," they say, "I want to get close to a woman, but no, I don't want to make a commitment now. What's the hurry? I'm not going anywhere."

At the same time, the women in their age group are saying, "How long do I have to wait?" "Am I wasting my time?" "Why can't I move in *now*?"

• WOMEN AS PREDATORS •

Men fear entrapment and smothering relationships, but they need intimacy also, even though they are experts at disguising it. In the sixties, everyone was into self-fulfillment and doing their own thing. The seventies took narcissism to new depths. In the eighties, narcissism and alienation are no longer perceived as healthy—or even cool. Society expects men and women to pair off in monogamous relationships.

Yet there is still that terror that I hear in the voices of young men. The ones who haven't been married have been told horror stories by their married friends. The ones who have been married and divorced, say, "I don't want to be locked in again. I don't want all that fighting and trauma."

As soon as women start circling and cutting off their escape routes, men panic. What are they getting roped into? While they want the closeness, they want the distance, the freedom to bolt when they choose. In the movie "Fatal Attraction," after the married male hero sleeps with the single woman villain for the first time, he leaves a note and goes home. Although his wife is away, the hero doesn't want to stay in the single woman's apartment for the night. He comes into his own place, opens the refrigerator, and the phone rings. The men in the audience jump and let out a collective groan. They know it's *her*, the woman he just went to bed with. They are supersensitive to entrapment, to the wily tricks of women who want to ensnare them.

The hero of "Fatal Attraction" never deceives the woman he has the affair with. He never tells her he's going to leave his wife and marry her, or that he's interested in anything other than a brief weekend fling. Yet she pursues him relentlessly, feels abandoned, has a psychotic break. She is an extreme example. But men tell us that women don't listen to news they don't want to hear. Even if they tell them, "This isn't permanent," they continue to make assumptions. For a woman, a weekend is a step toward permanence. For a man, it may just be a weekend *period.* He can send flowers and care about her, but still not want a permanent arrangement. Women have trouble understanding this.

Renee told us that Harry, the forty-year-old dentist we had introduced her to, was sending mixed signals. "He never said anything about being serious, but he kept inviting me to his country house for weekends. We went on Easter vacation to the Club Med with his daughter. Doesn't that sound serious to you? I don't think I can go on waiting for him to make up his mind."

Harry told us, "I thought I made it clear that I don't want to get married again. I don't know what the problem is."

Men can separate the two things: commitment and weekends. Women are usually not as compartmentalized. Actions and emotions flow together. If he takes me on a vacation with his daughter, he must be auditioning me for the role of her stepmother.

After all these years, I have learned most men try to be honest. But they don't always make themselves as clear as they think they do. Harry knew Renee had marriage in mind, and he probably never said he *would* marry her. On the other hand, he never said he *wouldn't.* He wanted the relationship to go on just the way it was, so why should he clarify it?

Patrick *does* want to get married, and his

mistake, he told us, was putting that on the table too soon. Nina started acting as if it was a fait accompli after the sixth date. She started taking over Patrick's social life, rearranging his furniture, making plans for the future. "But, my God, that woman was bonding all over the place, before I had a chance to take off my hat," he told us. He pulled the plug as fast as he could.

What A Woman Can Do:

It's not unusual for women to become nervous about the status of the affair and begin to press for closure. That's when guys begin to feel trapped, and start to check the exits. Men tell me the worst mistake a woman can make after a few dates is to start planning for the future. The future should be next week. Don't think any further ahead than that at first. Wait awhile before you try to pin him down, and then do it with extreme caution.

If a woman needs to know where she stands, she has to say to the man in a nonthreatening way, "Look, we've been seeing each other for six months. What do you want? How do you see this relationship developing?" But don't try this after six dates.

• WHO'S AVAILABLE FOR A COMMITMENT? •

Let's back up a little. Before a man or woman who wants a long-term relationship gets involved with a person of the opposite sex, he or she should get an idea if this is a viable candidate. At The Godmothers we rate men and women by the degree to which they are available for a committed relationship. By their responses to a series of questions and tests we can predict whether they will be susceptible to a long-term romance. We rate them C for Counterfeit, B for Borderline, and A for Available. In a pilot project of 150 clients, 100 percent of the clients who got a C rating dated the person they were introduced to only a few times, and try as we might to come close to the person they said they wanted, we were unable to match them with anyone they continued to see.

People who received a B rating were good for the short sprint. They saw the person they were matched with for three to six months before the bubble burst.

Ninety-nine percent of the A clients dated for six months or more. In a follow-up study a year and a half later, we found that 45 percent of the Available clients had married another client of ours, 12 percent had married someone they had met on their own, 26 percent were still dating the person we'd introduced them to, and 8 percent, having dated the client we introduced them to for six months or more, were now seeing someone they'd met on their own.

Only two Counterfeit clients in the study had married (one remarried an ex-spouse, the other married someone he'd known for six weeks, and divorced her nine months later).

Here's a profile of an Available person:

1. Timing: They are free of past entanglements and have come to terms with earlier failed relationships. Most have reached a point in their careers where they have time to spend with someone else.

2. Flexibility: Available clients are willing to modify their demands for ideal partners. For example, they might ask for a nonsmoker, but if everything else is perfect in the profile of a potential date, then they are willing to give it a try. We have found that the less ready a person is to settle down, the more rigid are their demands.

3. Self-perception: Available people have a more realistic view of themselves than Counterfeit ones. They are aware, for instance, of how they are perceived by others, and of what their true assets and liabilities are.

4. Perception of others: After an initial date we get feedback from clients. Their reactions help us select the next date, but they also reveal whether they are Available, Borderline, or Counterfeit. Availables are more generous and willing to give someone a second chance. Borderlines can be talked into one posi-

tion or another. "Oh, he thought I was terrific? Hmm. Well, maybe I would like to see him again." Counterfeits are always disappointed. They are obsessed with petty details and dissatisfied with everything.

Obviously, you can't give men a test to see whether or not they are open to a committed relationship. So how can you spot men who are not ready to settle down? Here are some signals to look for:

1. Pass up men who say they don't want a relationship. If they say it, they mean it. Men don't kid about this. We know a man who is now fifty, who has never been able to let a woman get too close to him. He always tells a new love that as soon as he feels he's becoming too involved, he bolts. They listen, but pay no attention, because they figure it will be different with them. Things go beautifully for six months or a year and then he gets anxious and splits. The last time the terror struck him, he left some of his clothes at the girl-of-the-moment's apartment and was so spooked he never returned for them.

2. Don Juans naturally are a bad choice. A man with a history of "loving 'em and leaving 'em" is okay for a vacation fling, but not for planning the future with. This one never changes.

3. Men who have recently broken up or have been divorced from another woman are too shaky emotionally to know what they want. Give those wounds time to heal before you lose your head. Or if you insist on seeing someone in this condition, give them a long leash and keep your expectations on ice.

4. Avoid men who talk about "needing space," "needing time," or being a "loner."

5. Any man who tells you that his previous relationships ended because the women wanted commitments is not a good bet. But we've seen men like this suddenly flip, so don't let go too quickly. Just don't use the *C* word.

What A Woman Can Do:

The time to evaluate whether or not a man is available for a commitment is *before* you fall in love with him. If he's not available, you can avoid becoming emotionally involved with him. That's easier to say than to do, but slowing down the pace of involvement will serve two purposes. It will give you time to find out as much about him as possible, and it will keep him from panicking if he is rushed.

Monitor the situation and enjoy it for now, but don't expect it to go on forever. Everyone brings their own agendas with them. A lot of women ask "Am I wasting my time?" too soon. If the last three affairs didn't work, they tend to despair and set up another no-go situation by pushing too hard or turning sulky.

• TIMING IS EVERYTHING •

Henry is forty-five, divorced, the father of two children, one of whom lives with him. He likes sexually exclusive long-term relationships. "I didn't think sleeping around was a great idea, even before AIDS." He had been seeing Margery for about a year, and since he liked her a lot, it seemed like a good idea for her to move in. But that didn't mean he was ready to marry her.

"Now I see that Marge moved in too quickly. I let it move to the next level too soon. I didn't lie to her. She's the best woman I've ever known, but I told her that living together didn't mean I was going to marry her, although it was always a possibility. She's thirty-seven and she wants to have children, so she started pressing. I realized I didn't want to be married. I don't want any more children, and I see now that I don't want to be married to her.

"Women are more realistic than men. Once they've seen what they want, it's easier for them to make a commitment. She's moving out as soon as she can get her apartment back. I'd like her to stay, but she's focused on getting married and having children."

What happened to Henry was that he couldn't make the transition from short-term to long-term bonding with Marge. Short-term bonding and long-term bonding is a concept developed by sociologists Lionel Tiger and Robin Fox. Short-term bonding is the intense feeling of first love that makes you want to be with that person all the time, that burns with a bright sexual flame. You focus on the merits of the loved one and disregard the defects. There is a euphoria of closeness and intimacy. If reciprocated, this stage can last up to three years.

The next stage comes with a sudden jolt of reality. There is a waning of the original sexual excitement, and an awareness of all the irritating and disruptive traits that were ignored before. If the couple can bridge the transition, they move into long-term bonding. The sexual attraction is less intense. Each partner has a more realistic view of the other, and knows what they can depend on and what they can't. They can build a genuine, loving, caring long-term relationship.

It used to be that people would court for a year or so, marry, then a year or two later the honeymoon was over and the problems would start. Today, when a couple has a committed relationship for a year or so, they come to the end of the short-term bonding, and some like Henry can't make the transition to long-term bonding—at least, not with that person. One person, in this case Marge, says, "Hey, let's get married, let's buy a house, let's have a baby." If she or he doesn't move on when the partner doesn't bite (as Marge is), and hangs around, the relationship usually slides downhill, because it doesn't have what it takes to develop into long-term bonding. It doesn't grow; it just wears itself out.

Since it's women who seem to have the responsibility for monitoring the progress of a relationship, when is the right time to check it out if you are still in the dark? I have found that most men won't volunteer a progress report. They may not have thought about moving in together, or they may be reluctant to suggest it because of a fear of rejection. They are afraid to say they won't marry you; and they're afraid to say they will marry you. Either admission is too confining and final. But if asked about any of the above, they will try to give you an answer. The trick is to find the right time to ask, and to ask in the right way.

What A Woman Can Do:

Alan was taken with Sharon, an exercise instructor at his health club. They went out on weekends and had a great time. Then she wouldn't hear from him for days. Finally, Sharon sat down with Alan after one of their dates, and said in a nonthreatening way, "I want you to take some time to think about whether I'm just another girl in your life or if there's something special about me. I find it confusing to have you blow hot and cold. I just want to know where I stand." No scene, no hysterics. Just a quiet request for an evaluation.

Alan thought it over for a week and decided

this woman *was* special. When he told her, it changed their relationship. At the beginning, he had been trying to keep himself removed. He wasn't sure where he wanted to go with it, so he held back. Once he realized he wanted to make a commitment, things got much better. The closeness brought a new intimacy and fulfillment. The timing had been right for the change, for an acknowledgment of what they meant to each other, and once that was in place, the barriers crumbled.

• THE ULTIMATUM •

An ultimatum is different from a request for a status report. It's a demand for closure and a threat to end the relationship if there is no commitment made. Bonnie worked as a copywriter in an advertising agency. She'd been seeing Drew for three years. They had separate apartments, but spent weekends together, and often saw each other on week nights, too. They spoke on the phone at least one or twice a day. Their parents took a liking to each other and they had all fallen into the habit of being together on holidays and birthdays.

Bonnie was thirty-five, and she didn't care much about her job. She hated her studio apartment. What she really wanted was to have children and to live in a nice house. Drew always said things like, "Give me more time," or, "I want my career in place." Finally, Bonnie gave Drew an ultimatum. If he didn't marry her, they would have to stop dating, because she wanted to get on with her plans for her life. He tried to stall for more time, but Bonnie was firm. Drew bowed out. They still talked on the phone, and their parents still saw each other socially, but Bonnie went about the serious work of finding another man.

She started dating a high-powered lawyer in another city. He was forty and had never been married. He began to take up more and more of Bonnie's time. After a year, he wanted her to come to live with him. It was difficult to do in the light of what had happened with Drew, but Bonnie issued another ultimatum. She wasn't going to give up her job and uproot herself unless he made a commitment to marry her. He didn't much like being put in that position, but he realized she was the perfect mate for him, and that it was time he started on the family he had always wanted.

Why does an ultimatum work at times and not at others? I always tell women who ask my advice that it works when a man is ready to commit. If he isn't ready, it won't work. Premature demands for a decision can backfire. "If he loved me, wouldn't he want to marry me, as much as I want to marry him?" It doesn't translate that way. He can love you but still be afraid to undertake the responsibility of marriage. Bonnie's first friend, Drew, loved her, but he was unwilling to give up his options and settle down. Her second friend had sown his wild oats and built his career. He was ready to get married. But I do believe an ultimatum is more effective sooner rather than later. If there have been arguments and bad feelings, it's a tired subject and the barriers are up.

Hunter runs an inn in a small New England town. Sally and her two children had lived with him off and on for four years. It was a stormy relationship. Sally made herself useful in running the inn, but she nagged and was moody. She desperately wanted some security for her children and herself. Hunter understood that and was sensitive to her needs, but he was worried about the financial and emotional commitment Sally expected. He was afraid of what would happen if she really left him for good, and hated his dependence on her.

Every so often Sally left, but she always came back. After one particularly bitter fight, Sally took the children and went to her mother's house. This time, Hunter was relieved to have her gone. He never would have been able to ask her to leave, but he was tired of the arguing and discontent. He started dating an attractive divorcee who had just moved into town to take over a property that had been left to her by the death of her grandmother. In two months they were married. She doesn't help Hunter at the inn, but he's hired a competent manager, and finds he can get along nicely without Sally and have more fun.

What A Woman Can Do:

If you're going to make an ultimatum, be sure of your timing. I generally advise women to wait at least six months to a year, or as long as it takes, for both of you to be aware of your feelings for each other. Be careful about waiting too long and giving the situation time to deteriorate.

Be sure you can stick to your resolve to end the relationship if there is no commitment, whatever your definition of that is. This is not an exploratory probe. You should already have done that and exhausted other avenues of discussion. This is an extreme measure, and not to be taken lightly.

Be firm but friendly. Open with something like, "Our relationship doesn't seem to be going anywhere," rather than putting him on the defensive with an emotional blockbuster. Give him a reasonable amount of time to make up his mind. And then—and this is important —be prepared to act on your threat to stop seeing him. Move out or move on, but don't give him a second chance. If he doesn't make the commitment you want—to love, to marriage, to exclusivity—sticking around will only make you feel resentful and cause more erosion of the situation.

Either he will be shocked into a new level of recognition of how he feels about you, or the whole thing will fizzle. Don't count on his not being able to live without you. But if he can't, and you've hit him at the moment he is prepared to acknowledge that, your gamble has paid off.

• NOW OR NEVER •

I recently met a woman in her early thirties. She said she was tired of men who wouldn't make commitments. Her new strategy was to withhold sex until a man agreed to marry her. And how long did she think that would take? "They should know that in two months," she said. I don't know how her plan worked out. It used to be effective before the sixties, when courtship didn't automatically include sex. The dating phase, however, often went on for a year or two, then the couple "went steady" for another year or two, then it could be another year or so before an engagement was announced.

Today, men have too many alternatives to be captured by that kind of tactic. "If I'm not going to get any, I'm moving on," said one of my clients about a woman who wasn't responding to his sexual come-on. And that pretty much sums up the prevailing sentiment.

It's a mistake to even think you can force or trick a person into making a commitment when he isn't ready or willing to. A more practical strategy for the woman who wants a committed relationship is to try to screen out unavailable men, and then to have the best time of her life with the one she's dating. If she's made a mistake, and he's not available, then at least she's had a good time and can go on to the next one with renewed zest.

• Chapter 7 •

Assessments

At The Godmothers, we don't exactly type-cast men and women, but we do find it useful to assess what kind of personality category they belong in. Assuming that a man is genuinely in pursuit of a relationship, and that his pathology doesn't trip him up, he knows instinctively what kind of woman is compatible with his type. Our job is to match up his vision and ours.

Most of us have characteristics that drive some people up a wall, but that others find adorable. Do you like men who are extroverted or contained, racy or bookish, good providers or do-gooders? The trick is finding out what a person is all about, including whether or not this is someone who is capable of the kind of relationship you're looking for, and then letting him know you well enough to come to the same conclusions.

133

• HOW TO JUDGE A MAN •

How do you tell whether he's Mr. Wonderful or Mr. Bad News? You have to be alert to all the signals that can give you clues. We started giving men a nail polish test. We'd ask, "Do you prefer women who wear nail polish or women who don't wear nail polish?" Don't laugh. The men who like nail polish always turn out to be the power brokers who have car phones and party all night. The anti-nail polish men are more into lives of the mind or the outdoors. They take sabbaticals in the British Museum or go fly-fishing in Canada.

So when you meet a man, how can you figure out whether he's for you? Start with the obvious. Where does he live? How does he live? What does he wear? Surface behavior carries buried messages. Take the striped rep tie. John T. (*Dress for Success*) Molloy says that mobile venture capitalists and international lawyers don't wear striped rep ties. The stripes of the rep tie originally indicated belonging to a British military regiment, then to a university, and now perhaps to a nation. "The clothes of a worldly traveler are ideology-free," says Molloy. So a man who wears a striped rep tie would tend to be a traditionalist and centered in his own community, rather than a citizen of the world.

Or take a man who wears a blazer or sports jacket and pants to work. He's probably self-employed or in a position that doesn't require conformity to a corporate suit culture. If he's also wearing loafers instead of lace-up shoes, he's definitely positioned himself in the freer world of academia, advertising, or independent entrepreneurship.

Does he live in an ascetic studio apartment or a splashy townhouse? Is his kitchen as ship-shape as a galley, or a messy invitation to urban wildlife? If you're twenty-five and not living in a penthouse, this doesn't mean that you won't aspire to one later on. But if you're twenty-five and not neat, you probably never will be. One of our clients told me she learned a great deal from a visit to a new date's apartment. He had a more than comfortable income from a family business, and yet at age forty he was still living like a kid just out of college with little better than a cot for a bed, a rickety dinette table and chairs for dining, and unfinished bookcases for his huge library. "It sure looked to me like a case of arrested development," she said. "It helped me to put his whole personality into perspective. I thought he was hung up on the past, and when I saw his place, I understood everything. He had a lot of old garbage to get rid of before he could get on with living a grownup life. I have done a lot of missionary work in my day. I knew at once that I wasn't going to stick around to try to convert this one."

You can't quiz a man the way we can, but you can ask questions about his previous relationships and family that will reveal all kinds of clues. When he talks about how his last relationship ended, he says, "I still don't know what that woman wanted." The little-boy-lost pose could be put on to get sympathy. Or he might be one of those types who's so busy sending messages that he never receives any.

Or when questioned about the breakup, he says, "I'd just as soon forget the whole thing." He may be covering up something painful, or he may be emotionally withdrawn, but in either case, he's established that he has difficulty communicating on an emotional level.

He has a live and let live attitude toward his last relationship. This is a man who has no need to blame himself or the next woman about what went wrong before. He shows promise of having a secure sense of himself and a genuine liking for women. If he has nothing but negative things to say about the women in his life, watch out.

The point of trying to establish his personality profile is to see whether or not you can cope with it—and whether he's worth it. This isn't like a medical diagnosis. Neither medicine nor tender loving care is going to make much difference. You shouldn't assume that you're going to be able to change him. Particularly beware of trying to reform the depressed, the misogynist, or the alcoholic.

• THE AGES OF MAN •

Personality types don't totally change at different ages, but sometimes they recast themselves. A person's needs and goals shift, and they are willing to assume different roles. Perhaps they want a different kind of mate. A man who has passed through two wives and two families said, "I have children with people I don't know anymore." He and the wives of the old marriages have followed such different paths that they are strangers. Another older man who was too wrapped up in his career to spend time with his family now wants to start a second family and pay attention to his children. He is in transition from being a workaholic power broker to becoming a more centered man. But chances are he will still need to keep a lot of the power symbols under his control, including the final say in how the children are raised and where everyone goes for vacations.

In our experience, men between twenty and thirty are more interested in getting married than women of the same age. Men are competing in business or their chosen field and would like to pair up with a woman who would be available and back them up, so they would have enough time to make their deals and be with their buddies. Women of that age often want to date older men who are established and more successful. They want to get on with their own careers. For them, marriage requires more of a time commitment to running a household than they can afford at that stage.

Of course, many men do find partners and marry by the time they're thirty. When women reach thirty, they start to look for marriageable men, and find they're either married or have had their first divorce and want a few years of freedom, or that they're looking for younger women to date. A man over thirty who hasn't yet married is often shell-shocked by the traumas of dating, and not sure he can ever trust a woman enough to marry her, or he's settled into the single lifestyle and becomes a professional single. He's so used to being the chosen one, and living a life with no responsibilities, that he's freaked out by the thought of being tied down. Besides, if he's ever going to make a mark in his chosen field, this is probably the last chance for it to happen. Maybe, he decides, he'd better concentrate on his career.

Men in their forties want something different than men in their thirties. They want to slow down. They want to stay home more. They don't feel compelled to run around. They might have arrived at a different level of sexual desire and proficiency. These normal changes in their sexual responses can lead to a crisis in their self-esteem or in an existing relationship. By now they are closer to wanting the same things as women, and are probably launched on their first or second marriage. They know and understand more about the mysteries of women that baffled them before. If they are looking for a mate, they are more mellow and flexible.

Men over fifty may be less flexible. Although we find that many older men are still open and questing, they're more apt to have succumbed to what I call "hardening of the attitudes." A person gets stuck in a routine. He goes to the same seashore resort every vacation, stays in the same hotel, and probably reserves the same room. His mind is patterned, too. He gives to the same charities and pushes the same lever on the voting machine every year. To a woman this might be frustrating, but it could also be comforting if she likes safe and predictable people.

A spirited more adventurous woman we know, who's in her fifties and who's seeing a man in his sixties, chafes at his sedentary and immovable fixations. "He didn't want to go to Turkey with me on an archaeological tour, because he thought everything wouldn't be air-conditioned or something. He won't even go to the beach with me, because he doesn't like to get sand on his feet." But, on the other hand, he's supportive, adoring, and dependable—qualities she appreciates after being married to a man who, while a better traveling companion, was often not there for her when she needed intimacy or emotional support.

The notion that older men are looking only for younger women is overrated and overemphasized. Because wide age differences between a dating couple are so noticeable, people remember when they see a sixty-year-old man with a twenty-two-year-old woman. Sure, lots of older men do want younger women, even though they're sometimes embarrassed to admit it. They'll say, "I want a family," instead of coming right out and confessing that they're turned on by young bods. But we find that men over forty are just as apt to want women their own age as women who are younger. Some older men say younger women make them feel energized and alive. Others say they are looking for someone closer in age because they have more of the same life experiences. A man who's been a mentor once too often doesn't want to be worn out by someone at a different stage of development. And if they don't expect to start a second family, they don't look forward to being pressured by a younger woman who has children on her mind.

Within the variables of age, here are some of the personality types we see most often and what you can expect from them. The idea is to evaluate how your own preferences and foibles match up, and what life with someone who answers this description would be like:

The Recently Burned: This describes a condition that is temporary and so the Recently Burned man is not a true type. He is really a type in transition. If you spend time with a man who has recently broken up with a woman or has just divorced, be prepared for someone who is experiencing pain, discomfort, or anger in some degree. He is not himself. I have clients who say, "I won't go out with a recently divorced man." Well, by the time he's less recently divorced and stabilized, he'll be taken. We know of one desirable man who was in such bad shape when his wife left him, that he didn't seem to care about any of the women he knew or who were introduced to him. A couple of women who tried to cheer him up and to lure him out of his shell were stonewalled. He needed someone who was all sympathetic ears, who would just listen to him. The woman who did get him? His shrink.

My advice about a Recently Burned: If you like the guy enough to listen to long, intimate conversations about what went wrong, and how he feels about it, hang in there. Don't spend all your time with this person, but don't entirely dismiss him.

Power Broker: He defines himself in terms of his ability to get tables in restaurants, and how he's evaluated by those he considers his peer group. He's aggressive and dominating. He assumes a "take it or leave it" stance with the women in his life. He wants the final say on how to raise the kids, where to go on vacations, and how often to see your family and friends. He's interesting when he's on top, but let him lose his membership in a club or his latest acquisition, and you'll find yourself with a depressed and unhappy person on your hands.

He's good for women who want power by association, and who don't mind non-negotiable limits on their activities and opinions. There is usually something seductive about so much raw authority. But beware, he might view you as a recent acquisition and may not be able to develop any more intimacy with you than he did with his last stock purchase.

Impossible Dreamer: Here is someone who never quite puts it all together. In his life there is always a new dream or scheme, which falls flat before it gets off the drawing board. He often wants to combine two qualities or goals that are mutually exclusive. Like he wants you to be successful in your work, but he also wants you at home with his dinner ready. You can recognize him because he's usually held a succession of jobs that never quite work out, belongs to Utopian organizations that stage marches and demonstrations, and has trouble organizing a simple evening out.

With an Impossible Dreamer, the journey is always better than the destination. He is a good match for a woman who has her own mission or wants to do good. If your roots are in reality or you have different priorities, after a while you may have difficulty suspending disbelief. And he doesn't thrive with doubters.

Makeover Man: He is a perfectionist, like the client who gave us a detailed list of the qualities he wanted in a woman and then complained, "I like long, tapered hands," when we introduced him to a woman whose fingers were too short for him. He often fancies himself a Pygmalion who likes to actually make over the hair, clothes, and tastes of the women he dates. Generally he goes for women who are much younger than he is, the more malleable the better.

Dating a Makeover Man can be a trip for a woman who thinks of him as a mentor she trusts. If she has lots of potential and she wants some direction in developing herself, this is perfect. One problem is that this Pygmalion gets tired of his Galateas once he makes them over. The other problem is that most of the makeover artists aren't nearly as appealing as Professor Henry Higgins in *My Fair Lady.* Once she's just the way he wants her, she gets bored with him. Chances are, she'll leave him for a man who accepts her just the way she used to be.

But we've known successful makeovers. Martin is thirty years older than Trudy, whom he hired out of Stanford Business School to be his assistant in a small computer consulting business he ran out of his apartment. He taught her to manage the business, to be his hostess, to read the right books. This was more than a cosmetic conversion. He always said she'd leave him once she'd learned everything he had to offer. But she didn't. One reason is that he keeps reinventing himself as well as everything he touches. Perfectionist, yes. Boring, no.

Loner: Picture a quiet, introspective man who needs lots of time to himself. He is "inner-directed," that is, he marches to his own drummer, is self-reliant, often intelligent, with a quick wit and a wry perspective on the world.

Some loners are friendly, but need to balance their together-time with alone-time. Some, however, just don't like people that much. They resist going to parties and are impatient with small talk. They need someone who doesn't get affronted by their frequent withdrawal, and who has her own agenda. A bicoastal arrangement is good, but a dual apartment setup works, too. He might include you in his life if you give him enough space and don't rush him. Look at it this way, it's better than being tied up with a womanizer. You know that when he's not with you, he's not with anyone.

Angry One: This guy has a lot of axes to grind. He's angry at his parents, his former spouse, his boss, and he's rude to everyone. Listen when he talks. Does he blame all his problems on his father who didn't have the good sense to make enough money to give him the advantages of a prep school education and a ticket to Harvard? Does he drag out the bones of his failed marriage and throw them at his ex-wife?

Does he lump all women together and come to the conclusion that they're all greedy, selfish, and untrustworthy? Except you. You're different, he says. That makes you feel terrific. You are special. This man is impossible to please, but he's singled you out for a dispensation. He's not angry at you now, but this story always has an unpleasant ending. Sooner or later, he will turn his wrath on you. It's a temptation to think that you can make all the hurts go away, that you can mellow out the anger, but you can't. If you grew up in a combative household, however, and you don't find yelling and screaming threatening, you might be able to live with it. In fact, if fighting is your thing, here's your open invitation to do battle. We've found that the Angry Ones like women who will stand up to them. Fighting alone is no fun.

Diamond in the Rough: Max is in the trucking business, thirty-eight, a self-made man. His suits look as if he slept in them and his five o'clock shadow seems to start at high noon. But he's generous and sharp, and he's looking for a serious relationship. Max is a Diamond in the Rough. He was looking for someone who was heavier on looks than brains, and we found him an occupational therapist with a great heart and a sense of humor.

These macho men who've come up the hard way either want someone to feel superior to, as Max did, or they're attracted to classy women. We fixed up one couple like that: He was a surgeon who came from the wrong side of the tracks and had never picked up the polish he realized he wanted. She was from a more advantaged background, but was open and flexible. He was a fast learner and she was looking for some stability in her life. It was a match. A Diamond in the Rough can be a good bet for a woman who likes to take some risks. But you have to be sure to distinguish a

Diamond in the Rough from a Zircon in the Rough. They're *all* risk and no relationship.

Mr. Limelight: Your function as a date is to be the audience. You can spot this ego junkie easily because he asks nothing personal. His questions are confined to, "Do you like my new suit?" and "Which movie do you want to see?" If he does slip and ask something about you, answer fast because his attention will have wandered before you get to the second sentence. He never makes an effort to find out who you are, because he doesn't regard women as people to have two-way conversations with.

This type believes sincerely that women are an energy drain, so he distances himself. He's looking for a live-in mistress and housekeeper whose role is to relieve him of mundane details and to be the stage he tap dances on. Anyone with a strong ego need not apply.

Excitement Junkie: This is an instant romance man. He rushes in where angels fear to tread —and may rush out just as fast. You'll feel smarter and thinner after a few weeks with him. But he's usually a short sprinter and then on to the next. He's looking for a good-time girl and no sad songs about commitment. There may be something deeper here, but he keeps it well hidden.

No matter what his flaws are, you're going to have a good time with him. He likes to hang glide and go to glitzy parties. He picks a livelihood on the edge—he's a commodities trader or a stunt man. He's wonderful if you've ended a relationship and feel down. He might be just the thing to give you energy and get you going. Approach the Excitement Junkie with no expectations but for the sheer fun of it, and you'll have a terrific time. Everyone should order at least one from the Chinese menu of life.

Centered Man: This is the type for the long haul. He has a sense of responsibility to his family and friends. He loves his work and the people around him. He makes everyone look good and feel good. This is someone who even calls his mother so often she never complains.

He has good judgment that gets him through life in an unscathed way. He's unneurotic but not uninteresting. Instead of wasting his energy in nonproductive ways, he has plenty for tennis, travel, and all the good things in life. He's looking for an evolved woman and he can skip the surface glitz. Give him uncomplicated and generous. Women who are used to emotional cripples may find it difficult to make the transition to someone so well adjusted and giving. No, he doesn't have any ulterior motives for being so nice. Grab him if he walks in your door.

Retro Man: He can be twenty-five or fifty-five, but he's unaware that the fifties are over and that we're now in the eighties. He's in a time warp. He wants things the way they used to be.

He's never heard of the Women's Movement or Vietnam. We had a client who was a Retro Man who came from a close family. He was a real estate developer and employed his brother. Patrick was thirty-nine and looking for an old-fashioned girl to take care of. This was a man who *expected* to take care of a wife. He wanted her to stay home and raise the children and run the house. Patrick liked the school teacher we found for him and they dated for awhile, but she became impatient with the slow progress of the affair.

Retro Men tend to move deliberately. But they want to see you more and more instead of less and less. They don't open up quickly, but their lives and personalities gradually unfold if you are patient enough. And they don't change their minds once they're made up. Loyalty is one reward of moving back in time with them.

The Victim: He can be quite charming and irresistible. It's not until later that you begin to see the pattern: He's always casting himself in the role of the fall guy. It was his secretary who messed up the report, his publisher who made the book late, his insurance agent who steered him wrong so that he's not covered for the theft. Then it begins to dawn on you that he never acknowledges responsibility for any of his life tragedies. Someone else *always* causes the trouble, and then he uses his misery to get attention and sympathy.

He has no gratitude, and never praises or

thanks anyone for their help. He is entirely focused on people doing him wrong. Not that he doesn't trot out his endearing side once in a while to keep a woman interested. He can be so witty and winsome, so clearly in need of help and understanding, that you're hooked all over again. When he holds out hope that the right woman could make him happy and fulfilled, you start to believe it's true. Don't count on it.

Emotionally Absent: Women can be emotionally absent, too, but we are more used to seeing men who can't relate to others on a feeling level. Some of them are blissfully unaware of what's going on with other people. They are so self-involved that they don't relate to the turmoil or needs of a live-in lover or wife. Then there is the type who is an emotional cripple. He goes through all the motions of concern. He takes you out to dinner when you're blue, but he doesn't really relate to your problems. It is as if he is hollow inside.

The first type has possibilities. His potential for emotion is intact. He just isn't in touch with his feelings, because he doesn't think it's manly, or because that was the way people acted in his family. It is conceivable that he could learn to touch his own emotions by trying to understand yours. The emotional cripple is probably too frozen inside to be thawed by an amateur. He needs to be motivated enough to want to get professional help.

But maybe you are attracted to this kind of

man because you don't *want* someone more emotional. Maybe the distance is what you can safely handle yourself. Some women are more comfortable with a situation in which there is no two-way emotional exchange. That would make a good fit with an Emotionally Absent man. He wants feelings coming from you, and he may be responding in his own way. He may show his emotions through actions, not words. Consider your own history of selecting partners before you give up. Are you thinking that all men are emotional illiterates, or are you just attracted to those who are?

The Givers: Givers come in two varieties—give-give and give-take. Give-take appears to be generous and outgoing. He is like one of our clients who described himself as being "a nice guy, good, maybe too good. I try to please too much." He gives too much because he needs a lot of approval and attention. While he's giving away all the goodies, he's also taking all the bows. He provokes rejection because he is so obviously needy. This person wants no enemies or criticism so he just keeps trying harder. But deep down he resents his dependency on everyone for approval.

He needs a woman who is no threat to his fragile ego, someone who will accept his largess at face value and ask no questions when he plays Santa Claus. She has to be smart enough to anticipate his anxiety about making a mistake, so that she can cover for him. Maybe she should be a give-give type.

The give-give type is also heavily invested in making other people happy. But he is more adept at muting his need for applause than the give-take. He has more confidence in himself. He is often ambitious and competitive, likes to solve problems for people—even if they don't want him to. He is really an easy guy for most people to get along with, although some women wish he would be more vulnerable and honest about his needs. He gathers a lot of wounded people around him whom he tries to nurse back to health. Occasionally he falls in love with one of them, but this doesn't work out because he eventually feels taken advantage of. What he really needs is a strong woman who will instinctively give him what he doesn't ask for.

• FINDING MR. WONDERFUL •

These are some of the types we come across in our daily work. Men talk to us and we try to understand what they are saying. If women will listen, they will hear the unspoken messages, too.

The most productive thing a woman can do is to analyze her own type. If you know what your needs and desires are, it makes it easier to find your Mr. Wonderful. But don't narrow your options by rigid requirements. If you're always looking for richer, taller, older, smarter, the same religion, the same race, the same sports, you'll sleep alone a lot of the time.

The least productive thing a woman can do is to paint her fantasies onto a man. No matter what this woman hears, she sticks to her own agenda. A successful decorator I fixed up with an architect kept hoping he would try to fit into her lifestyle of charity balls and society teas. Even after he turned up at a black-tie dinner in a Mao jacket and sneakers, she kept expecting him to buy a tux, but he was never going to.

At The Godmothers we see that you can't change the basic structure of another person. It's like trying to teach an elephant to waltz. You can make it more graceful, but it's still an elephant. It's better to make a cannier match in the first place. If you need graceful, start with a gazelle. Or better still, take another look at elephants. You can count on their loyalty, which might turn out to be better in the long run than pairing up with a good dancer.

• Chapter 8 •

Friends Or Lovers

"**A**bove all, she's a good friend, and that's more important to me than I would have thought possible." "She's my best friend. I can tell her anything." Are these men talking about the girl next door, or the Platonic buddy they go to the movies with? No, they are talking about their current steadies or fiancées. I hear more and more men bragging that their lover is also a friend, and more men are asking us to find a woman for them who will develop into a friend as well as a romantic interest. This is a late eighties' phenomenon that I think will develop and grow. It's as if the word is out to a whole segment of the population that they've been looking for love in all the wrong places.

It used to be that you made a choice: you were friends or you were lovers. The twain didn't meet. Maybe the revolution started with co-ed dorms, where boys who didn't have sisters woke up to the fact that women were people. Then there was all that impersonal sex that became a downer for a lot of men. And women demanding intimacy, that caught a lot of guys totally unprepared. Whatever. Men have gotten the message. Friendship is what they need in their lives.

Both single and married people seem to be trying to reinvent a way of relating. Men come to us asking for a date who can develop into a pal as well as a lover. Although looks are still important to them, they tell me they need someone to talk to, not just someone to take to bed. Particularly, men leaving their twenties behind begin to look for more enduring values in their relationships. It doesn't make sense to play musical beds anymore. It's too unrewarding—and dangerous. They want to get to know a woman better before making judgments, and then they want to forge more lasting bonds than their divorce-prone parents and friends. "You know, we really are reinventing the wheel," a thirty-eight-year-old divorced lawyer told me. He was talking about the woman he planned to marry. "My first wife and I were a lot of things to each other, but we weren't friends. It's so different with Laurie. You can't imagine how being friends changes everything."

• LOVE, HONOR, AND OBEY •

Friendship didn't use to be part of the marriage contract. When marriages were arranged, the bride and groom didn't even have to *like* each other. Even in our society of free choice, the idea of husbands and wives being friends didn't seem to occur to many people until quite recently. Sure, it happened in many good marriages, but it wasn't expected.

Today, the idea of lovers or spouses being friends still isn't exactly universal. A middle-aged man I know said to me, "I want a wife who's a wife, not a friend. I don't want my children to be my friends either. I'm their father not their friend. And I don't want a dog who's a friend. Dogs are animals, not people. A lot of people go soft on dogs and try to treat them like equals. That's why so many dogs misbehave. You really have to be clear about these things." This man wants to keep control of all his domestic relationships. Friendship demands equality and sharing. If you want to maintain a master-servant equation, forget being a friend. If you are playing The Autocrat of the Breakfast Table, the woman waiting on you is your wife *period*.

But friendship between men and women is possible today because they are increasingly considering each other equals. They go to college together and sleep in the same dormitories, they work together and have equal status on the job, they share responsibilities and have comparable mobility and independence. As men and women develop more parity, they find they really can be buddies.

Perry is twenty-eight and in the travel business. He was very specific about wanting to connect with a woman he would be comfortable with as a friend. "In college my best friends were women. I like to talk to them about my problems and what interests me. Don't give me a flirt or a flighty type. I want someone I can really talk to and who likes to travel. I hate to make trips alone, so a companion who likes the same things I do would be perfect."

Perry is not unusual. Many men have discovered that they want to relate to women on this level. But not only do they want pals, many of them want confidantes. Often men have said to me that it is easier to talk to women about their feelings than to men. Their male friends are great for going to a ball game with, but not to talk to about trouble with their boss or how worried they are about their mother. Men are too competitive with each other. Typically, they put the best face on everything rather than risk seeming vulnerable or needy with other men. With women it's different. Most women aren't going to judge them and find them wanting if they confess to some weakness. Women are used to being open about feelings. There is something in the female sensibility, no doubt cultivated by our society, that makes women more tuned into the nuances and value of the emotional life than men are, and so they are the perfect companion in times of stress or disappointment, when a fellow wants to let his hair down.

Another reason men have found women are good to talk to about their worries is that women can be nonjudgmental. They'll just listen and not try to pontificate or offer advice that's not wanted. The new man is often looking for a woman who will be a financial partner and share economic responsibility with him. Now he's saying that he'd also like another kind of partner, one to share the traumas and doubts with, too.

What A Woman Can Do:

Men really want a woman who's going to be a best friend, someone to conspire with them, listen to them, laugh with them. Developing a friendship with the man in your life isn't going to cut in on your sex life. It should only enhance it. Gone are the days when you had to make a choice between being a friend or a lover.

But you don't have to be his *only* buddy. We also hear from men, "Why can't a woman be more like a man, with great sex thrown in." One man wished he could talk to his girlfriend about his fantasies about other women, the way he does with other men. Another said, "She's great but she doesn't like to go to baseball games." No one can be all things to a person. That was one of the fallacies of the fifties, that a woman could fill every need for her family. Nowhere is it written that men who have a deep and abiding friendship with the women they live with should stop having other friends.

Encourage him to keep up his contacts with

male friends. Let him talk to men about his feelings about other women and let him go to the ball game with his male buddies. Equality doesn't mean doing everything in lock step. It means having respect for the individuality and preferences of the other person, and giving them time and space to develop them. That's what friends do for each other.

• BEST FRIENDS •

Every once in awhile I hear a man say, "I love her but I don't *like* her." What he usually means is that there is a strong sexual and romantic attachment, but they don't share the same values and ideas. That kind of relationship seems passé today. Men aren't separating the passion from the palsmanship the way they used to. Woman as a sex object is definitely on the way out. What is more commonplace is a yearning for a good friend who can also be a good lover.

A thirty-six-year-old teacher I know said to me, "I think I'm very lucky. I consider my wife to be my very closest friend. We enjoy doing many of the same things. But what is most important is we like to talk to one another. It's like when you are out in a restaurant and you look around at the couples. You can tell those who are married from those who aren't. The ones who are married don't have anything to say to each other. Even though we've been married for twelve years, we like to think that our level of talk is such that when people look at us they think we're a couple who aren't married."

Sociologist Robert Bell did a study in which he found that 60% of the men he surveyed considered their wives their best friends, and 50% of the women considered their husbands their best friends. More men need wives as best friends than women need husbands, Bell thinks, because men don't have as many friends outside of marriage as women do, and fewer have "best" friends. Their idea of a male friend is someone to do things with—go bowling or play cards with—but they don't have that many close friends. Women do. They have one or more "best" friends with whom they share not only fun, but also ideas and emotions.

Sportscaster Warner Wolf said in an interview, "Your wife is your only friend. When everyone else leaves, your wife will be your only friend.... My wife fulfills my needs. She is a real companion." We hear this over and over from married and living-together couples.

And this is what uncommitted men are hoping to find, too. They complain when it doesn't work out the way they want it to. We fixed up Carl, a good-looking young doctor, with Mary Lou, a fashion coordinator. They seemed to like each other and to be compatible, but after a few dates, when Carl wanted to spend unstructured time together, when they could talk and get to know each other better, Mary Lou was restless. "She's always suggesting a movie or a business party we could go to, or something, anything, so we won't be alone together," he told us. A call from us alerted her to the problem. "Look," we told her, "Carl wants to spend time with you with no particular agenda. He wants to develop a friendship. Just relax and let it happen." Mary Lou took the cue and instead of trying to develop her career or her entertainment portfolio when she was with Carl, she concentrated on getting to know him and letting him get to know her.

Another sign that he wants you to be his friend: He talks about his career and his plans. When a man is with someone he thinks is too lightweight to understand what's going on in the important areas of his life, he steers the conversation to other topics. But if he starts to open up about subjects that are vital to him, he is beginning to trust and reach out. This is a signal to a woman to listen carefully and to reciprocate with a discussion of her own plans and dreams.

He tries to interest you in the things that interest him. One of our couples seemed to have everything going for them, but Susan missed her chance when she repeatedly refused to join Les in the play-reading group he enjoyed so much. He had been meeting with the same group of friends once a week for a few years. Once a year they actually staged a play for a select, invited audience. All he asked was for Susan to sit in a night or two to see whether she liked it. She kept saying she was too shy to perform in public, and even though Les explained that she wouldn't ever have to go on a stage if she didn't want to, and how informal the readings were, she wouldn't take the risk. Not too long after that, Les started to date a new woman who came into the play group, and he stopped seeing Susan.

What A Woman Can Do:

Remember that many men want and need friendship with their partners more than women do. Women who are aware of this and try to be supportive, will be rewarded with a deeper and more satisfying relationship. Be sensitive to his outreach and to the signals that he's trying to be your friend. When he wants to share his work and friends with you, his passions and thoughts, treat him the way you would a female friend—with understanding and responsiveness.

And speaking of female friends, don't abandon your female friends when a man comes along who wants to be your friend, too. This is never an either-or situation: Either you get rid of them or you'll lose him. Make time in your life for both. Perhaps you won't be able to see your female friends as often as you used to, but they will understand as long as you keep in touch. He will respect your independence, and the fact that you don't rely on him to fulfill all of your needs. Besides, after that male lover has departed, your female friends will still be there.

• JUST FRIENDS? •

They often have romantic candlelit dinners in quiet restaurants where they sit completely absorbed in their conversation. They once worked together, but don't any longer. Still, they talk on the telephone at least once a week about mutual friends, business, gossip. The couple I'm describing aren't lovers and never have been. They are "just friends." He's married. She was when they first knew each other. After her divorce there was some sexual tension between them, but they decided that wasn't the way to go. I've talked to both of them and they admit that there's just a teensy bit of sexual attraction still there, but neither one has ever tried to act on it. They appreciate the benefits of the relationship they have and want to keep it that way.

Nonsexual friendships between men and women are more common among young people. But when single young adults begin to focus on either long-term sexual liaisons or marriage, friendships they have formed with a member of the opposite sex are usually jettisoned. In our society we seem to be able to accept sex without friendship but not friendship without sex. Having a friend of the opposite sex outside of the marriage implies that something is wrong with the marriage.

Fortunately, though, at a time when families continue to disperse, and more adults need all of the close ties they can muster, many men and women do continue to be friends even after one or the other forms a close relationship with someone else. I often hear a man say, "I think she's terrific, but I don't want to marry her. I want her as a friend." Or after the romantic relationship comes unglued, both parties decide they want to maintain the friendship. One man I know prides himself on having kept up friendly relations with all of his ex-lovers. He often invites them to be guests at his country house, gives them advice and support with their problems with current lovers, and generally plays big brother when he's needed.

Saying to someone that you want to keep them for a friend after the flame of love flickers out is a kinder way of ending an affair than just pretending the whole thing never happened, or going away mad. And as a bonus you get the continued company and rapport with someone you care about. A "friendship declaration" can also turn around an affair that doesn't seem to be going anywhere. One of my clients told me that after she and the man we'd fixed her up with had been seeing each other for a few months, she was feeling neglected and confused. He said he was interested in her and didn't seem to be seeing other women, but his calls were erratic and she was never sure when they'd have the next date. Finally, one night she told him, "I find it difficult to go on in this sporadic fashion on a romantic basis, but I don't want you out of my life. I'm really very fond of you, and I'd like to continue to have a close friendship with you."

He was visibly shaken by her friendship declaration. For a minute he was speechless. Then he said, "But I want you to be more than a *friend*." For the first time they talked frankly about what was happening between them, and from then on the romance really blossomed—alongside the friendship.

What A Woman Can Do:

Smart women are learning to hang onto men they like and to incorporate them into their lives as buddies. Maybe the romance fizzled, or perhaps it never got off the ground as scheduled. Well, if it's someone who would enhance your life, don't dismiss him too cavalierly. Tell him, "I don't want you out of my life. I want a close friendship with you."

A thirty-eight-year-old museum curator told me, "A lot of people think I'm peculiar because I have so many male friends who are close. If there was a sexual part to the relationship, that is past and we stay friends. In fact, I think I hurry through the sexual part, so we can have the friendship. Some are married, but it doesn't hurt their marriage. I'm not sure how many tell their wives how close we are." That's probably a good way of getting the next partner of either of the friends to accept the friendship. Just don't talk about it too much or in glowing terms. There are, after all, still taboos about having friendships with the opposite sex outside of close relationships.

• SUCH GOOD FRIENDS •

Men and women who are afraid of love because of a fear of rejection, unsettling surprises, loss, hurt, are probably afraid of friendship, too. If they won't risk putting themselves on the line for a romance, chances are they're going to have problems with developing friendships.

People who come to us and say they're lonely usually have trouble forming relationships of all kinds, including friendships. One way of discovering what you are dealing with is to ask a man about his friends. Daphne met a strong, silent type, a chemist. When she asked him whether he had friends, he said, "Lots." It turned out, however, that he saw some of his friends once or twice a year and the others every five years. This is not an unusual concept of friendship for a man to have. Despite her misgivings that he would have trouble relating to her, Daphne found herself falling for the guy. But she was right, it wasn't an affair made in heaven. Usually, but not always, the kind of man you can have as a romantic friend has friends. He might want a different kind of friendship with a woman, but at least you know he has the capacity for being responsive to overtures of friendship and the outreach to keep it going.

What are the things men look for in a friendship with a woman? First, trust. He has to know he has found someone he can depend on to keep his secrets, to be understanding and compassionate when he makes mistakes, to stick by him during rough times. Men say, "I want to be able to talk off the top of my head without worrying whether she's going to blab about it to someone else, and I want someone nonjudgmental who's not going to monitor everything I say and then throw it back in my face."

They definitely don't want an adversarial relationship. Nothing upsets them more than women who talk about how terrible men are. "Don't give me a woman who's angry at men. As soon as something goes wrong, she'll lump me in with all the other men who did her dirt." A woman who is going to dump all her past bad experiences on a man isn't going to make a dependable friend.

One of the things men ask for most frequently is a woman who has time for them. Friendships with either sex take time and persistence. People who are successful at making friends are considerate about intruding, but don't stand on ceremony. They make an effort to stay in touch and to make themselves available when they're needed. A guy might think it's unmanly to ask for help when he's moving, or for compassion when his dog dies. A friend takes the time to drop by to see what can be done without waiting to be asked.

Men usually like women to ask *them* for help. Not that they want an old-fashioned, helpless female. But most of them enjoy being asked for advice about a financial investment or to lend a hand in putting up a new bookcase. If, however, your man isn't responding to this kind of friendly overture, back off gracefully.

Don't give unasked-for advice. As one man put it, "In a way friends are like family, but with one important difference, they don't constantly give advice the way your parents do." *Vive la différence!*

What A Woman Can Do:

It's helpful to think about how you behave with your women friends. Men don't expect any more from you than your women friends do. They don't want to be unfairly criticized or nagged or made to feel guilty. People tend to be more permissive with their friends than with their lovers. They often take better care of a friend's feelings than of a lover's. If you want to make your lover into your friend, a wise strategy is to treat him with the respect and kindness, the openness and forgivingness that you extend to your women friends.

• THE STRONGEST BASE •

I find that both men and women are more cautious with each other than ever. They are both being guarded and tentative these days. Even a man who doesn't want to be alone anymore is afraid of taking that leap toward intimacy. He doesn't tell a woman that he's being protective. He probably doesn't even know it himself. If he's had one love affair too many, he's sour about the whole idea. Or if he's waited too long for "the real thing," he's worried that he won't recognize it when it comes along.

One way out of this impasse is friendship. Columnist Ellen Goodman said in an interview, "I would say that the strongest and most trustworthy base of love is friendship. If you love someone you like, you're in a lot better shape than if you love someone you don't like. You tend to hang in there longer."

I think many relationships break up because friendship is missing. I hear, "She was great in bed, but we had no common interests." "She was fun to be with, but we weren't emotionally close." One divorced man came to us and said that now that he and his wife are divorced and they have no sexual relationship, they've become friends. But he wants both. He was looking for a woman he could be sexually close to *and* who would also be his friend.

"Soulmates" comes up regularly. When a man says that, he's really talking about friendship. Friendship is a way of opening the door to closeness and intimacy, of forming a long-term bond that can weather disappointments and imperfections. If you have a person who is a friend as well as a lover, you will wake up one day after the fireworks of first love die down, and find you have someone to talk to.

• Chapter 9 •

What Men Want
(And Don't Want)

After all these years of matchmaking, I can almost predict what men will ask for in a woman—what pleases them and what will drive them to distraction. Sometimes, of course, what a man requests is not what he really wants. A client in his early forties asked for a fun-loving woman. When we found one for him, he sheepishly admitted after the first two dates that she was too frisky for him. He'd just come out of a messy divorce and thought he needed bright lights and big times, but bar hopping, parties, and late nights turned out to be more like punishment. And then from time to time a man walks in the door and orders the impossible: A tall blonde who's twenty-two, has blue eyes, plays tennis, loves her job, and reads Sanskrit. We don't even touch that kind of shopping list.

Mostly, though, the patterns are clear and within reason. Men ask for certain characteristics and complain about others with amazing regularity. Styles and trends come and go. Requests for nonsmokers and wholesome types, for instance, have been big in the eighties. But there are constants that don't seem to vary with geography or the fad of the moment.

• WHAT ATTRACTS MEN •

The first thing men tell us they want is a woman who's bright. By this, they mean they are looking for an equal partner, someone who won't be dependent on them. She should be resourceful, flexible, intelligent, and have her own interests and job. "I don't want a woman who depends on me to make a life for her," said a new client whose business requires a lot of travel. "I'm really looking for someone who has her own ideas and isn't going to wonder about what she's going to do when I go out of town. My last girlfriend used to act injured when I traveled a lot."

This woman should also be someone dependable whom a man can count on to ride out uncomfortable times, or to take over in an emergency without making a federal case out of it. It shouldn't be a sacrifice for her to move his car into the garage if it looks like snow. One fortyish man told us that when his mother was dying in another city, he left his son with his live-in girlfriend so that he could go to his mother's bedside. The girlfriend kept picking fights with the son, which he had to mediate on the telephone every night. That was the beginning of the end for him. He couldn't tell her about his disappointment, he just began to distance himself. "What could she do to change, if she wasn't mature enough to handle a situation when I needed her to act responsibly?" he asked.

Ah, but this wonderfully independent, reliable woman should also be available. As one insurance executive put it, "She shouldn't be so caught up in her career that she won't have time for me." This is a recurring theme, too. Men have found that the "bright" women are the busy women with an agenda of their own. No matter, they want her to be independent and to also make time for them when they want it; that's their fantasy.

The next quality they all want is a sense of humor, not dancing on the tabletops humor, but someone with a sense of fun who isn't overwhelmed with angst all the time. The men who ask for a woman with a sense of humor don't necessarily have one themselves, but maybe that's why they need someone to lighten up their lives.

Another thing that's attractive to men is a down-to-earth woman. "Don't give me someone who puts on airs or is phony." They want a solid, grounded woman, not a flighty, flashy cream puff. Give them someone with old-fashioned values and virtues. The ideal woman of the late eighties is "wholesome."

All the men in the world seem to have ganged up on aggressive women. They say it any number of ways: "No ball-breakers," "I don't want any pushy types." But what they mean is the same. Interestingly, women equate aggressiveness with achievement and ask for men who are aggressive, dynamic, and successful. But men don't make the same connection. For them aggressiveness is threatening and impossible to live with.

How To Attract A Man

1. Go places alone. You are more accessible and available that way.
2. Take your children or your dog. They place you in a context, and they're good ice-breakers.
3. Have fun. Men want to be with women who are having a good time.
4. Be friendly. Keep building bridges. Who knows where they'll lead.
5. Be adventurous. Climb a mountain or tackle French. Take chances.
6. Don't rely on props like a book that make you inaccessible for conversation.
7. Don't be timid at parties. Make the first move.
8. Don't feel rejected if a man doesn't respond. There'll be another one along in a minute.

• ATTITUDE •

No one wants to take on a friend or lover who's going to make him feel bad. It makes good sense to avoid people who bring you down. Men are looking for an upbeat person with a sense of self-worth. But they want more than that. Men are saying, "I want someone who will take me out of myself." Sure, they're afraid of desperate women, but what they want goes beyond that. They want the kind of optimistic woman who is happy with herself and her career, and who can do the heavy lifting for both of them if necessary.

Another kind of attitude we hear a lot about is man-bashing. Men do not want to have anything to do with women who are down on men. This includes: women who say disparaging or ugly things about ex-spouses or lovers, women who lump them in with every man who ever did anything mean to them, women who have a chip on their shoulder for undetermined reasons.

Playing damsel-in-distress once too often is like crying wolf once too often. No man loves a loser. He expects a certain amount of competence from the bright and independent women he favors, so learn how to do a few things for yourself. It's okay to ask him to help you hang a picture or two, but coming off as needy and/or lazy can sound the danger alarm.

Lest women think men want women to subjugate their own personalities or to turn into "yes people," a word of caution. That's not what we hear them saying. What they ask for is a self-starter who has the ability to surprise and please in unexpected ways. Someone who becomes subservient to a man's every wish or cultivates all of his interests becomes as provocative as a used sponge. Men hate it when a woman takes on all of his characteristics, sports, and opinions. One young man we know is ambivalent about the woman he's been seeing for the last year, but he says, "Whenever I start thinking about wanting the freedom to go out with other women, she comes up with an idea that just knocks me out. Then I think, I'll never find anyone like that."

• THE PRESSURE COOKER •

For many people stress is a constant companion. Men tell us that they don't need any more pressure in their lives. They don't want to consider taking on a woman who's going to remind them that they haven't made it to vice president yet, or that happiness is a new cabin cruiser. Wrong. Wrong. Wrong. He's making as many demands on himself as he can handle, and he doesn't have to send out for more.

He is also very sensitive to women who want to get married *now* because they are rapidly approaching forty. Don't panic because your biological clock is ticking. You may make foolish decisions if you feel pushed, and you certainly will drive men away if you make *them* feel pushed. Men have their antennae out for this kind of coercion. Even the cleverest end run will probably not get by your average alert single man.

A man will often react negatively to even the most unobtrusive kind of demand. "Remember to take your keys." "Call me when you get there so I won't worry." "Why can't you pick up your clothes instead of throwing them on the floor?" All of that fussy stuff reminds him of his mother, who was overly possessive and domineering. Just the mention of it brings back all the maternal pressures he's been trying to cut himself off from over the years. He might temporarily welcome a surrogate Mom, but ultimately he'll have to split, just as he split from the real Mom.

A thirty-eight-year-old divorced engineer told us he'd just broken up with a woman who had seemed at first to be an answer to his prayers. She got along well with his daughter, and when she came to visit she would babysit if he wanted to jog or run errands. She cleaned up his apartment and cooked for him. But gradually she seemed to take over every aspect of his life, and began to expect to be with him more and more. He said the pressure was unbearable after a while. "She *seemed* to want to do all of this because she was unselfish, but the subtext was that she expected me to marry her, even though I told her I wasn't going to marry her." Instead of being grateful to this woman for her outpouring of generosity, he began to feel guiltier and guiltier. The breakup was unpleasant for both of them.

• CRIMES OF PASSION AND INDISCRETION •

Here are some of the deadly sins of passion and indiscretion that men tell us they hate:

1. Tears—For some reason, a crying woman makes a man feel helpless and acutely uncomfortable. He wants to run the other way, but that would be admitting how frightened he is, so he tries to tough it out. It's all so irrational, and confirms his worst suspicions about the unreliability of women and the imperfection of man.

2. Jealousy—Unprovoked jealousy can be flattering, as when she thinks that blonde at the party was flirting with him. But if she makes scenes about it, all the fun goes out of the game. It's humiliating for most men to be with women who are always patrolling. He's talking to someone new and pretty, and suddenly she's standing at his side waiting to be introduced. Any manifestation of free-floating jealousy can cause big trouble.

3. Overly critical—It's one thing to say to him, "I like you better in your blue suit," and quite another to say, "You have lousy taste in clothes." A little honesty goes a long way. Guys feel as if they're being attacked personally when the suggestions or criticisms have barbs in them. Male ego can be as fragile as the female one. One rule of thumb: Ask yourself, would you say something like this to a female friend? If not, then it's too cruel to say to anyone.

4. Snooping—They were getting along just fine, until Bob caught her looking at his

engagement calendar. "Why are you doing that?" he asked. "I wanted to see who you have dates with," she answered truthfully. Her candor saved the day, but Bob began to feel more guarded and watchful of her attempts to pry into his life. It changed the relationship in a subtle way. Men usually prize their privacy and actively resist assaults on it.

5. Inherited anger—Men can't deal with women who are carrying around ancient hurts and grievances. This goes for a woman who still resents her parents and blames all of her problems on a mother or father. Or one who is still talking about all the terrible things her ex-mate did to her. The best advice we can give you is, for your own sake, get rid of old anger, even if you need professional help with the exorcism.

6. Daddy's girl—I get a lot of negative feedback about women who want to be taken care of. Sure there are some men out there who want to be Big Daddy, but mostly Little Girl Lost doesn't play well on the big stage.

• WINNING LOOKS •

Likes attract. We even find that matching men and women who resemble each other works. I always tell a woman to dress to attract the man she wants. A button-down shirt and a wraparound denim skirt will say Preppie. A dark conservative suit with a feminine blouse will say Serious Professional with a frivolous side. If you look flashy, you will attract a flashy man. If you look fashionable and expensive, you will attract a man who can afford expensive women (and probably scare off those who can't).

I had a divorced client who was smart and had a responsible, high-paying job, but she complained that she kept attracting married men or sleazy operators. When I took one look at her I understood why. She had teased hair that was too obviously bleached, grossly false eyelashes, and wore overly revealing dresses and spike heels. I told her as gently as I could that the kind of men she wanted to go out with asked for women who were more conservative than she appeared to be. She resisted the idea of a makeover, but eventually she took a chance and toned down her look. Happily she found that when she looked like what she really was—an intelligent, high-achiever—she began to date men like herself.

Come-ons:

1. Men want women who are in good shape. No matter what else turns them on, trim and well exercised is a must.
2. Being well groomed is also essential. No man walks in and says, "Give me a woman who's well groomed." But if her

legs are unshaved or she's missing buttons, we hear about it. Too perfect, however, can be a problem for some. From them we hear, "She's so perfect, I'm afraid to muss her up." As far as they're concerned, tousled hair and chipped nail polish signal vulnerable and accessible. No Ice Maidens wrapped in polyethylene bags, thanks.

3. Men say they like women who wear no makeup. Actually, they don't realize that deftly applied makeup *looks* like no makeup, so what they really want is natural-looking makeup. No matter that it took you an hour to achieve that look, as long as it isn't visible to the untutored eye.

4. They appreciate clothes that are becoming and appropriate. They don't want you to show up in spike heels and a clingy black dress when everyone else is wearing blue jeans to the picnic. Many men have no memory for women's clothes. You could wear the same thing a hundred times, and if they like it, that's okay with them. One man often asked, "Is that a new dress?" This was puzzling to the woman he was dating because it often wasn't new at all. Then she figured out that this was his way of acknowledging an outfit he liked. They appreciate it if you have changed after work or at

least freshened up, to signal that this is a special date.

• LOSING LOOKS •

Each man has his own ideas about what is a turn-off or a turn-on for him. That's why women have to dress for success with the type they want to connect with. He's not going to be happy with Country Living if he wants Vogue. But within those parameters, here are the kinds of no-nos we get complaints about.

Turn-offs:

1. Hair that's windblown and casual can be erotic, but colored hair with roots showing or hair that needs a shampoo is definitely unsexy. We've seen a look of dismay cross the face of an otherwise tolerant man when a date showed up with hair that was so sprayed it looked freeze-dried. That he'll notice.

2. We've had men comment that a woman had a "lumpy" figure or that she was too "overblown." The problem was really clothes that didn't fit right and called attention to the wearer's worst points.

3. Some men say they find bow ties or running shoes with business suits comical. Not exactly the right position to be in if you want to be taken seriously.

4. The only comments we get about per-

fume are when the scent or saturation is overpowering. Perfume is one of those subliminal lures. Being too obvious breaks the spell.

5. "She made me feel uncomfortable," is what a man might say to us. If we press, we sometimes come up with specifics like, "She was always fidgeting with her hair, or dropping her earrings, or repositioning her fur coat to keep it protected or something." If you're not at ease with your equipment, he's not going to be either.

6. Putting on lipstick in public is another pet peeve. Also, women who keep looking in makeup mirrors in restaurants.

• TELEPHONE POLITICS •

The telephone is often the first contact a man and woman have, and it is certainly a big part of their communication ever after. Considering how important telephone behavior is and how much practice most people have with it, it's sometimes hard for me to believe the stories we hear.

A common problem is the person who brags when he or she is meeting a blind date on the telephone for the first time. Although it sounds like arrogance, self-aggrandizement can come from nervousness and a desire to please the other person. But when a man tells us the woman we fixed him up with said she looked like Margot Kidder, turned out to look more like Lily Tomlin, he's disappointed and mad. Rule number one: Don't try to describe yourself on the telephone.

Another blind date blunder is trying to guess what the other person is like. A barber who makes toupees told a *New York Times* reporter that one of his customers, a forty-five-year-old investment banker, was told by a woman in their initial telephone conversation, "You sound bald. I'd rather go out with guys with hair." At the end of the first date after an elegant dinner, the woman told the banker she'd like to see him again. He smiled broadly, ripped off his toupee, and walked out of the restaurant. Rule number two: Don't make any guesses about the other person.

Other mistakes we hear about: Dropping erotic innuendos and then playing hard to get. Men tell us about women who drop titillating come-ons about their sexual escapades from their end of the telephone, and then keep them at a distance when they try to collect. This is a major *faux pas*. That also goes for other exaggerations—name-dropping, trying to make your job sound more glamorous than it actually is, or otherwise embellishing your resume. And one more of the things men always gripe about: "I couldn't get off the phone with her!" Hang up while you're still ahead.

• SUCCESSFUL DATING AND OTHER GAMES •

Once you get past that first call on a blind date, then what? From the way men tell it, too many blind dates are disasters. Ron, a good-looking, thirty-year-old bond trader, said to me, "The reason I'm here is that I've lost three of my closest friends, because I let them introduce me to these women they think are perfect for me. They say I'm picky and difficult."

Then he went on to tell me about the last debacle. Jim, a friend who's an investment banker, wanted Ron to meet his boss's daughter. He said she was talkative and peppy, she had an okay body, and she was fun. "Well, I met her at the bar of the Pierre Hotel, which is pretty but quite sedate after 5:00 P.M. Lucille came in wearing a flower print dress brighter than the lighting. She gave the headwaiter a hug I would reserve for a more intimate relationship. I was already embarrassed. She was overweight and her cleavage wouldn't quit.

"After 20 minutes I was exhausted. Lucille hadn't stopped talking. She told me how cute she was. She told me people used her to get to her father. She told an awful joke. I didn't have enough energy to take her out to dinner. My friend was mad. If a blind date doesn't work out, the person who fixed you up defends the person they're closest to."

Gates, who's twenty-five and was interning

at a Boston hospital, had gone through a month of answering personals ads in the Boston *Phoenix*. He'd had a friend who'd met someone terrific that way and married her. "I don't know," he said. "Vivacious and spicy turned out to be a Yuppie with an overactive thyroid, the sophisticated, cosmopolite was a snob who thought she was God's gift to the world, and sensitive, good cook had the personality of a wet noodle and looked like she'd eaten too much of her own cooking."

Overselling or mislabeling doesn't make a blind date go more smoothly. But even first dates where the participants have at least a brief visual and maybe an inkling of what the other person's like, can be the pits, too. That sweet, little kid who was so helpful at the laundromat turns out to be a nonstop whiner, and the life of the cocktail party turns out to have agoraphobia and never goes out alone.

What do men hate on first dates? They groan about being dragged to parties where they're an outsider and don't know anyone—including the woman they thought they'd get to know better on the date. We also hear about the woman who keeps asking "Do you know so-and-so?" and then blathers on about people her date doesn't know or have any interest in ever meeting.

They have no affection for a woman who immediately tells them her wish list, and makes them feel inadequate. One client reported his date had dropped into the conversation that she's always coveted a second house in the country, that she's never met a Porsche she didn't like, and a wistful reference to the number of carats in her best friend's new emerald ring—all in the space of one hour. He disqualified himself immediately.

But spilling your marital goals is a worse gaffe than discussing your material goals. Men say that if they want to talk about marriage, they'll bring it up. "There's no such thing as an innocent mention of getting married," says one veteran of the dating wars. "There's nothing that puts me on the defensive faster than that delicate little foray into your deepest feelings about whether you're looking for a wife."

Another thing they don't want to hear the first night is the complete story of your life. If you cover all the bases, including your personal problems, there probably won't be a second night.

Men never ask us whether we think it's okay to go to bed with a woman on a first date. Nor are they disappointed if it doesn't happen that way. They tell us that they'd often like to try on the first date, but usually wait for a clear signal, which probably won't come for a few dates. "If nothing's happening by the fourth date, I usually move on," said one client, "because after that, it's probably not going to happen." When women ask for advice about the right time to have sex with someone, we say, "Remember, when you go to bed with someone, you may never hear from him again. Remember, also, that you may."

One of the most common complaints from men is: "She seemed distracted." If there's one thing men love, it's the undivided attention of the person they're with. They want the woman they're with to focus on them, not just with her eyes, but with her brain as well. "She seemed to close down at one point," men will tell me. "I wasn't getting through to her." "She kept working the room with her eyes. Even though she was responding with her mouth, I could tell her mind was elsewhere."

What A Woman Can Do:

Some women make up their minds too quickly about whether or not they have found Mr. Right. Ten minutes into a date they've already decided the chemistry isn't right. "Chemistry" can take time to ripen. Try to get to know this person first. You shouldn't be making a decision about whether he's "it" or not "it" on the first date—unless it's a complete fiasco. Once you've freed yourself from the burden of having to worry about what's going to come next, you can approach a date as a one-time, not a life-time, experience, and just have a good time.

At the end of the evening, if you'd like to see him again, say so. Men like to know where they stand. When they report in after the first date, they often say to us, "I don't know whether she liked me." They're afraid to make the next overture if they think they bombed. We can reassure a man that you did like him, but it's more effective if you do it yourself.

• DATA BANK •

Men don't make a habit of telling women what they want. They date them, bed them, smile, then leave for the next woman if everything isn't the way they want it to be. The bottom line is, they can't tell a woman she just doesn't fit into their lives, and they don't want to *change* her to make her fit.

As matchmakers, my staff and I help people by giving them information about each other that might be helpful. We had a client who called for his dates on a motorcycle; he had a car, but this was his strange way of testing women. To further complicate matters, he preferred traditional women who didn't fancy going out to a formal dinner party on a motorcycle.

Finally we fixed him up with a woman we knew he would like, but we warned her in advance, "He's going to ask you, 'Do you mind if we go on my motorcycle?' The correct and only answer is 'No, I don't mind.'" Once she had passed the initial ordeal by motorcycle, they traveled by automobile. If we hadn't cued her, though, she might have blown the opportunity.

You can create your own data bank. Ask your friends what they know about someone you are about to go out with. Do a little research on his work if you're not familiar with it. Ask nonthreatening questions when you're together, that give you a better picture of how his mind and emotions work, and store the answers for future reference.

Something can be said for packaging, but you have to know the man you're packaging for. Someone who wants a poodle won't be happy with a bird dog.

But it's also a mistake to focus too much on analyzing a man. Relax. Don't expect any more of men than you do of women. Don't worry about whether the relationship is going to work out. By paying attention and being your own best self, you have as good a shot as anyone—even better.

TACKLE LIFE'S PROBLEMS

With Help From St. Martin's Press!

HOW TO LOVE A DIFFICULT MAN
Nancy Good
_____ 90963-2 $3.95 U.S.   _____ 90964-0 $4.95 Can.

BEYOND CINDERELLA
Nita Tucker with Debra Feinstein
_____ 91161-0 $3.95 U.S.   _____ 91162-9 $4.95 Can.

WHEN YOUR CHILD DRIVES YOU CRAZY
Eda Le Shan
_____ 90387-1 $4.95 U.S.   _____ 90392-8 $5.95 Can.

HOW TO GET A MAN TO MAKE A COMMITMENT
Bonnie Barnes & Tisha Clark
_____ 90189-5 $3.95 U.S.   _____ 90190-9 $4.95 Can.

HAVE A LOVE AFFAIR WITH YOUR HUSBAND
Susan Kohl & Alice Bregman
_____ 91037-1 $3.50 U.S.   _____ 91039-8 $4.50 Can.

Publishers Book and Audio Mailing Service
P.O. Box 120159, Staten Island, NY 10312-0004

Please send me the book(s) I have checked above. I am enclosing
$ _____ (please add $1.25 for the first book, and $.25 for each
additional book to cover postage and handling. Send check or
money order only—no CODs.)

Name _____

Address _____

City_____ State/Zip _____

Please allow six weeks for delivery. Prices subject to change
without notice.